PLUGGED IN

PLUGGED IN

Keith Veronese
Author

Mark McNabb
Designer

Michael Kronenberg
Cover Designer

John Morrow
Publisher

Rob Smentek
Proofreader

TwoMorrows Publishing
10407 Bedfordtown Drive
Raleigh, North Carolina 27614
www.twomorrows.com
e-mail: store@twomorrowspubs.com

ISBN-13: 978-1-60549-047-2

First Printing • March 2013 • Printed in Canada

A full-color Digital Edition of this book (with bonus content) is available for $5.95 at:
www.twomorrows.com

PLUGGED IN

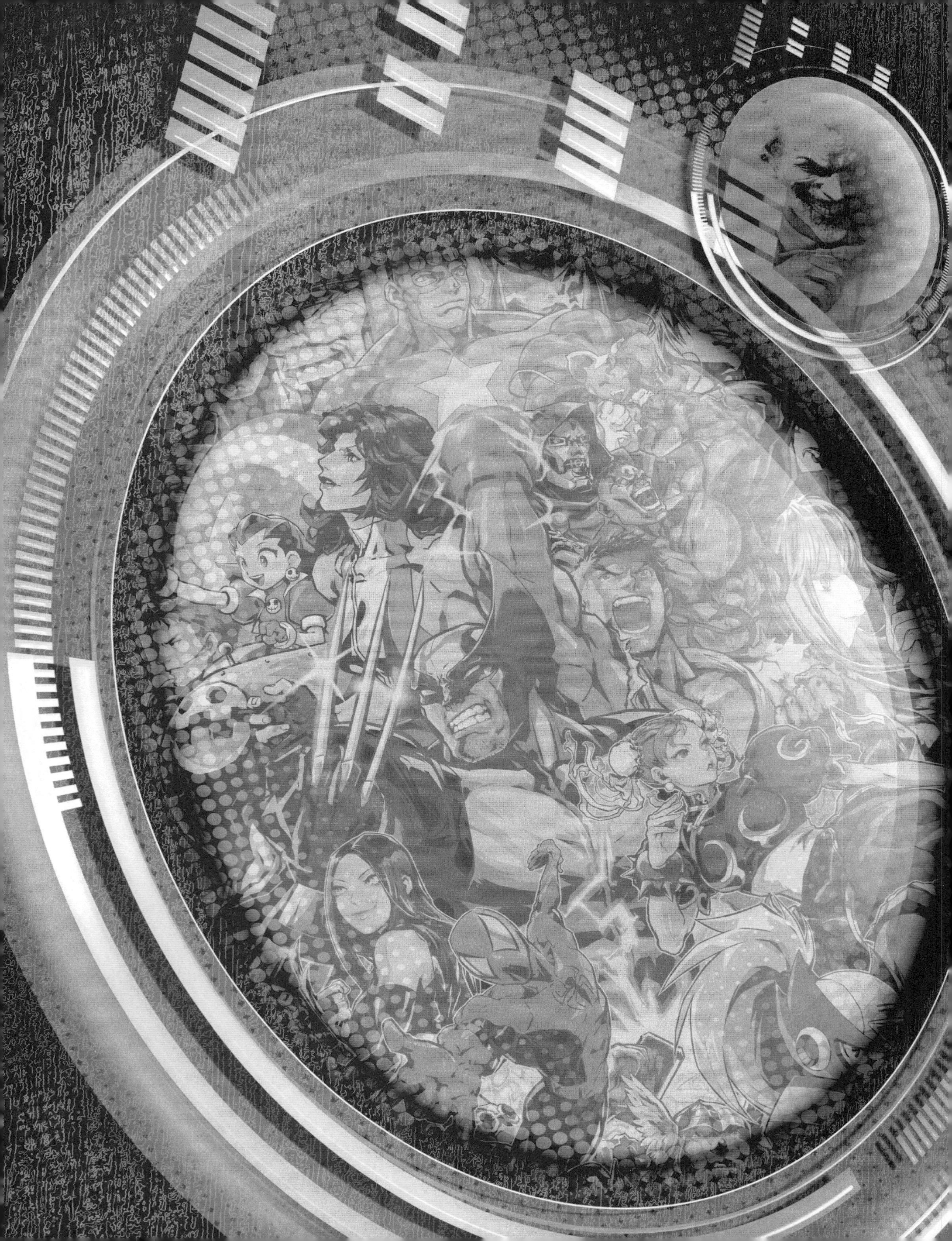

Fore**word**

Video games and comic books are 20th Century artistic ventures that have become mainstays of the 21st Century. In many ways, the rise of the American comic book parallels the rise of video games—unrivaled success in the Golden Age, a time of disarray leading to a rebirth in their Silver Age, and a period of rampant sales followed by contraction that led to an emphasis on high-quality storytelling.

Like comics books, video games went through a dark period akin to the early 1990s comic book explosion. Video game makers learned, the hard way, that it takes more than shiny graphics or licensed entities to ensure critical acclaim and sales success. This led many companies to delve into the world of comic books to seek out comic book talent and improve the quality and storytelling efforts of video games. Video game makers often revisit this "dark period" in a cyclical drive for graphical glitz and glamour with each new console generation, as publishers try to make the most of the new hardware and often letting story elements slide to the wayside. The first generation of games for a new console often sell well but lack staying power as they are quickly replaced by newer, more refined and balanced games.

Seeking out comic book talent to design characters, monsters, and craft the story of modern video games became common in the early 2000s. Several interviews follow that detail this process, as well as interviews with comic book veterans like Roy Thomas and Gerry Conway who entered the world of video games through a joint venture between DC and Atari in the early 1980s. These veterans provide interesting insights as they describe the rise and fall of Atari and console gaming in the early 1980s before the rebirth of console gaming in the late 1980s with the Nintendo Entertainment System, the Sega Genesis, and their successors.

Video games, due to their increased price and lengthy experience, have the opportunity to tell phenomenal stories, but the games often fail to do so. To make up for this, video game companies have sought out some of the best writers in the comic book industry to tell episodic tales and lend a sense of continuity to video game series.

In addition to viewing the role individual creators play, we will take a look at the evolution of comic book-based video games over the years. The first few efforts were quite dismal, with the comic book video games created as little more than cash grabs in the late 1980s. As titles like *Marvel Vs. Capcom 3* and *Batman: Arkham City* garner critical acclaim and sell millions of units, it is evident that this area of licensed video games has made incredible leaps in quality in a little over three decades.

Hopefully you'll learn something new about one of (or several) or your favorite comic book artists, as they work in a field that goes hand-in-hand with comics, but still lags behind in attributing contributions to those who worked on the games. This problem is similar to the attribution wars seen in comics in the 1960s and 1970s, but video games pose an additional problem due to the hundreds of people that work on a given project. The next time you beat a game, don't just skip over the credits and make a run for a drink or snack—you might miss out on learning that one of your favorite comic book creators played a role in your adventure.

Opposite:
Marvel Vs. Capcom 3 art

Batman: Arkham City game art

Above:
Batman: Arkham City game art

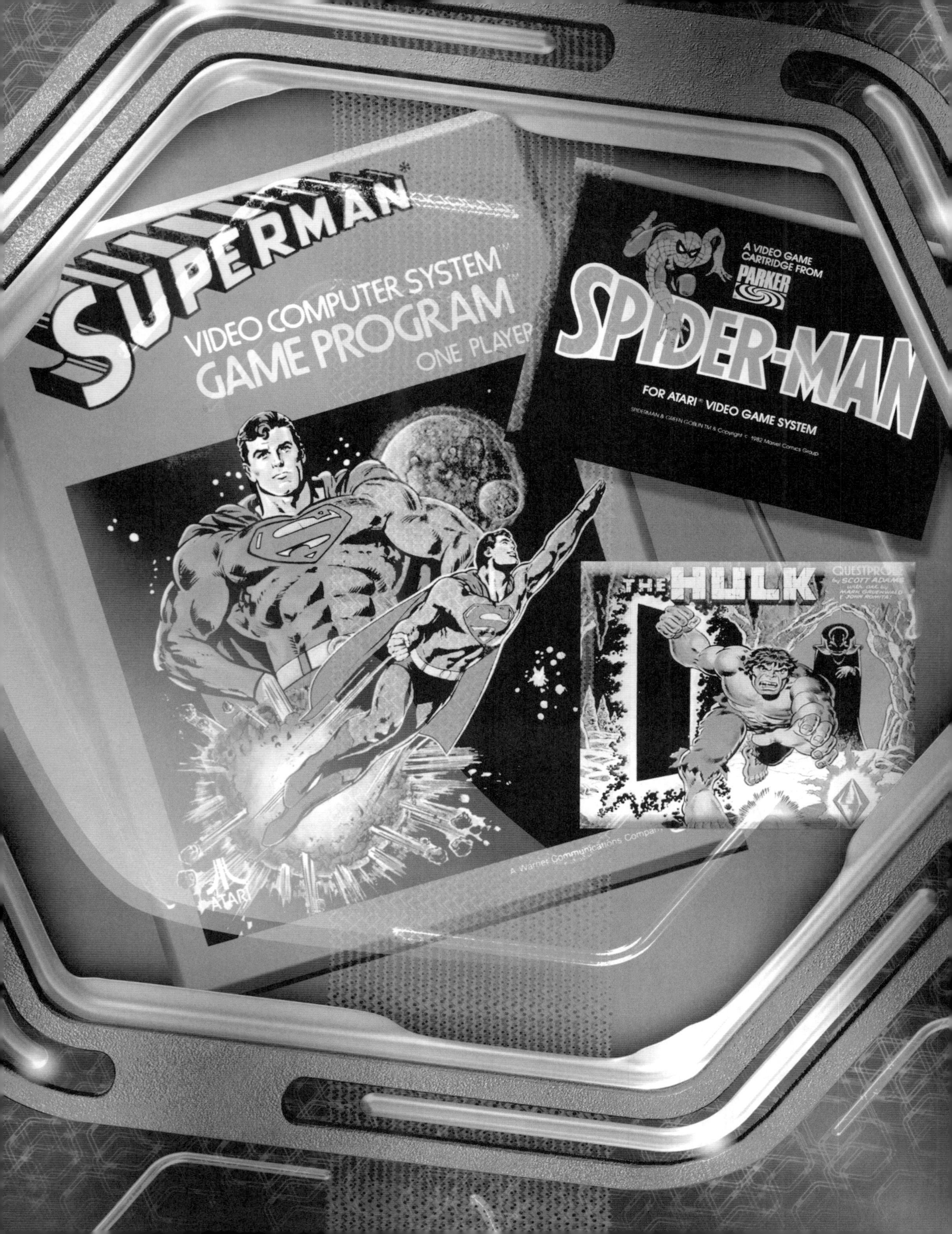
SUPERMAN*
VIDEO COMPUTER SYSTEM™
GAME PROGRAM™
ONE PLAYER
ATARI
A Warner Communications Company
A VIDEO GAME CARTRIDGE FROM
PARKER
SPIDER-MAN
FOR ATARI® VIDEO GAME SYSTEM
SPIDERMAN & GREEN GOBLIN TM & Copyright c 1982 Marvel Comics Group
THE HULK
QUESTPROBE
by SCOTT ADAMS

REBOOT:
Comic Book Characters Make their Way into
VideoGames

Comic books and video games. Both are mainstays of adolescence for the past several decades, stalwarts that have survived the days of our youth to become mainstream entertainment for people of all ages. However, only in the past several years have their talent pools mingled, allowing for video game creations with the quality and depth of story necessary to convey the comic book experience.

The Early Days

The earliest comic book-based video game is 1978's *Superman*, created by Atari for the Atari 2600, followed four years later by Parker Brothers' *Spider-Man* for the same system. Neither games are anything to write home about, as both games feature blocky, nearly indecipherable graphics, but then again, that's about all that was possible with the processing power of home consoles at the time. The graphics did not bother gamers, as they were happy to imagine themselves in the role of their favorite comic book heroes. In the three decades since Atari's *Superman* effort brought comic book characters into the world of video games, many things have changed, with one DC-licensed game seen as the gold standard for not just comic book video games, but video games in general.

One of the first successful tie-in venues pursued in the early days of video gaming, Scott Adams' *Questprobe* series, was released in 1984 for the Atari 800 and Apple II. *Questprobe* used well-known Marvel characters to appeal to the home computer gaming crowd. The *Questprobe* games mixed Al Milgrom's art with Scott Adams' design and story for a series of three games starring Spider-Man, the Hulk, and the duo of the Human Torch and the Thing. Marvel produced a *Questprobe* three-issue limited series, which features work by John Byrne, Mark Gruenwald, and John Romita. The *Questprobe* series marks the first effort to create a comic book that tied in directly to a video game. A fourth game and comic was planned, featuring the X-Men, but it was never released due to the bankruptcy of the *Questprobe* video game publisher, Adventure International, during the video game industry collapse of the mid-1980s. The comic art created for the

Opposite:
Superman, Spider-Man and Questprobe video games

Top:
Superman game screenshot

Above:
Questprobe comic

fourth game saw the light of day in *Marvel Fanfare #33*.

Console Frustration

In the early days of console gaming, manufacturers often sought ways to artificially increase the length of game in order to give the feeling that the gamer received more play time for their hard earned money. Home console video games hovered around the $50 mark during the 1980s, with games only now reaching into the $60 level. Adjusting for economic fluctuation paints a different picture—the 8-bit cartridge purchased for $50 for your Nintendo Entertainment System (NES) in 1987 would cost nearly $95 when adjusted for inflation. Unlike comic books, video games have come down in effective price over the past couple of decades, a trend that will likely continue thanks to the move from cartridge based software to DVD/Blu-ray technology and possibly completely digital distribution in the future.

In a shrewd move to sneak comic book characters into mainstream video games, video game developer Sega would use unlicensed versions of Spider-Man and Batman in their 1989 Sega Genesis game *The Revenge of Shinobi*. Batman and Spider-Man served as "boss" characters in one level of the game. Marvel eventually gave consent for this free piece of promotion, but DC Comics did not. Sega retained the Spider-Man character and added a copyright disclosure, while they removed the Batman character from later releases of the game.

Marvel and DC did seek out their own licensees in the 8-Bit and 16-Bit generations of home consoles, but the produced games are not looked upon fondly. Early Marvel Comics licensee LJN made *Silver Surfer* for the NES extremely fast paced and difficult to frustratingly extend the playing

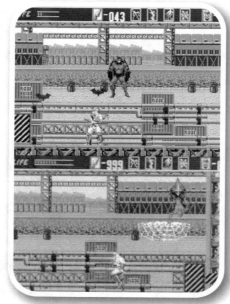

experience. LJN performed an even crueler trick for its NES release of 1989's *The Uncanny X-Men*. In the 1980s, automatic game saves via hard drive were non-existent, while battery-based cartridge storage added a considerable amount to the cost of video game production, so most video games relied on 20 to 30 character long strings of letters and numbers to return the player to the correct spot. To reach the final level of 1989's *Uncanny X-Men*, players had to enter a cryptic password. A single hint is given, with the answer located on the cartridge itself. This required the player to eject the game, find the code, and then enter a password to start the final level over again. One problem persisted—the code printed on the label is "+B+Up together with Start", however, the correct code to continue to the final level is "Hold Select+B+Up, then press Start." This frustrated countless gamers excited to play as the X-Men within their homes, and likely turned them back to simpler games like *Duck Hunt* or the latest incarnation of the *Super Mario Bros.* series.

While there were a plethora of dark points for console games and fans of comic books in the late 1980s and early 1990s, a couple of bright spots shined through. Sunsoft's *Batman: The Video Game* is still one of the high water marks for 8-Bit gaming, as it merges quality gameplay with accurate depictions of characters from the Batman mythos. The game's sequel, *Return of the Joker*, exceeded the original and provided a bridge between the 8-bit and 16-bit console generations by including an additional

Top to Bottom:
Shinobi's Batman and Spider-Man

Silver Surfer game ad

The Uncanny X-Men game ad

onboard processor within the cartridge to improve graphics.

Arcade Success

While console games were hit and miss during the 1980s and early 1990s, arcade games enjoyed much more success. Several video game companies looking to exploit the multiplayer possibilities inherent in team-based comic book games as well as the arcade goer's exposure to these known comic book commodities.

Taito released the interesting *Superman: The Arcade Game* in 1988, a game combining beat 'em up elements and shooting gameplay to simulate Superman's flight. The game stands out from a historical perspective thanks to the unexplained inclusion of a "red" Superman, a character with powers cloned from

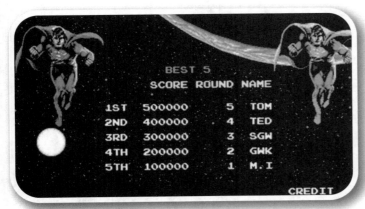

Superman that is often explained away by fans as an incarnation of Shazam or Legion of Super-Heroes member Mon-El.

While Taito's *Superman: The Arcade Game* allowed players to step into the shoes of Superman, Data East released one of the first successful multi-player comic book arcade games in 1991, *Captain America and the Avengers*. This quarter-eater allowed up to four players

to play at once, something arcades loved from a cash flow standpoint. Data East presented Captain America, Hawkeye, Vision, and Iron Man as playable characters with completely different sets of movements and abilities, a possibility previously unseen in arcades. Quicksilver, The Wasp, and Sub-Mariner stopped by to help out players along the way as the Avengers fought Juggernaut, Whirlwind, Sentinels, Ultron, Crossbones, and the Red Skull.

In 1992, Konami one-upped Data East's effort when they unveiled *X-Men: The Arcade Game*. This

six-player brawler allowed you and five friends (or arcade acquaintances) to take control of Cyclops, Colossus, Dazzler, Storm, Nightcrawler, and Wolverine, and slash through Sentinels, Blob and Pyro of the Brotherhood of Evil Mutants, and more before squaring off against Magneto on Asteroid M. Konami used images from the late 1980s cartoon pilot, *Pryde of the X-Men* to design the game, allowing the cartoon-style graphics to remain fresh and colorful to this day, with its enduring popularity resulting in a release on the PlayStation

Top Right:
Batman art and *Return of the Joker* packaging

Above:
Captain America and the Avengers ad

Left:
Superman: The Arcade Game

3 and Xbox 360 in 2010 and later for the iPhone.

From Side-Scrollers to Fighting Games

Capcom's quarter-eating sensation *Street Fighter II* paved the way for one-on-one fighting games in the 1990s, a type of game that pits player versus player in best two-out-of-three rounds combat to determine arcade supremacy. Midway's *Mortal Kombat* quickly

followed *Street Fighter II* along with numerous variations of both titles. Looking to take advantage of the popularity, Capcom released *X-Men: Children of the Atom* in arcades in 1994, using a very similar control scheme to *Street Fighter II*. Capcom followed up this release with the *Marvel Super Heroes* fighting game in

1995 and then the first installation of the now classic *Marvel Vs. Capcom* series in 1998. The *Marvel Vs. Capcom* series is a hit 15 years later, with *Ultimate Marvel Vs. Capcom 3* allowing players to take control of Marvel stalwarts Wolverine and Captain America along with obscure denizens of the Marvel Universe like M.O.D.O.K., Taskmaster, and a bizarre foe of both Dr. Strange and Conan, Shuma-Gorath. Marvel tapped comic artists Adi Granov and Mark Brooks to aid with the design of *Marvel Vs.*

Above Left:
X-Men: *The Arcade Game*

Above Right:
X-Men: *Children of the Atom ad*

Left:
Street Fighter II

Right:
Marvel Super Heroes arcade game

Bottom Left:
Marvel Vs. Capcom 3 art

Bottom Right:
Mortal Kombat Vs. DC Universe art

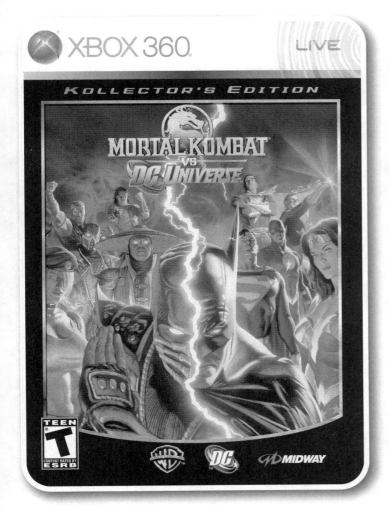

Capcom 3, with the duo lending their talents to promotional artwork and the game's final cover art.

DC Comics would try to replicate the success of the *Marvel Vs. Capcom* series by teaming up with Midway to create *Mortal Kombat vs. DC Universe*, but the extreme violence that accompanies *Mortal Kombat* games and DC's desire to not have their properties involved in such violence held the game back.

Improving Efforts on Home Consoles

While comic book-based video games achieved economic success, they were rarely at the top of annual video game rankings. Games featuring comic book characters often sought to tie-in audiences, which often shared a significant amount of overlap.

Just as comic book fans love crossovers, Acclaim published the intercompany crossover video game *X-O Manowar/Iron Man: Heavy Metal* in 1996 along with an accompanying comic book crossover. While the game itself is forgettable, it marks the first intentional comic book crossover between separate companies that extended into the realm of video games. Marvel and DC were not the only publishers to place their comic book commodities within video games. Games

based on independent and small-press series were prevalent, with *Cadillacs and Dinosaurs, Scud: The Disposable Assassin, Bone, Valiant's Turok,* and *2000 AD's Rogue Trooper* starring in their own games in the late 1990s and early 2000s.

Marvel's *Ultimate Alliance* series built off the initial success of the 2004 action role-playing video game *X-Men Legends*, an addictive game that allowed a single player to control up to four X-Men

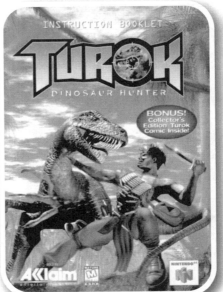

Above Left:
Mortal Kombat Vs. DC Universe packaging

Above Right:
X-O Manowar/ Iron Man: Heavy Metal packaging

Middle Right:
Cadillacs and Dinosaurs packaging art

Right:
Turok video game instruction book containing comic

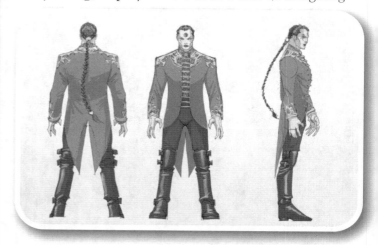

In the past decade, video game companies have sought out comic book creators, masters of graphic storytelling, to play a more active role in designing video games. Jim Lee worked on 2003's *Batman: Rise of Sin Tzu*, designing the main villain Sin Tzu, with DC hoping to later use the character in Batman continuity.

Sony Online Entertainment brought in comic book talents Jim Lee, Marv Wolfman, and Ale Garza to build a real life DC Universe for the massive multiplayer online role-playing game *DC Universe Online*, a game complete with new storylines that players could explore on a 24/7 basis.

THQ looked to penciler Joe Madureira (*Uncanny X-Men, Battle Chasers, Avenging Spider-Man*) to design

at once and level up to modify their mutant powers. *Ultimate Alliance*, took this to another level, opening up the entire Marvel Universe to players on the Xbox 360, PS3, and PSP. *Ultimate Alliance* allowed players to choose from over 140 Marvel characters and was chosen by Microsoft to be included for free in specially marked Xbox 360 consoles, opening up the Marvel Universe to a whole new segment of the gaming population. Marvel *Ultimate Alliance 2* debuted in 2009 and featured the popular *Civil War* crossover pitting Iron Man against Captain America that ran through Marvel Comics titles in 2007.

Video Game Developers look to Comic Book Stars

Modern video games give the opportunity to tell much more story than a single comic book or a graphic novel. These ten- to fifteen-hour couch excursions have improved in quality over the years, not just for comic book-based games, but games in general, as developers seek to form a high quality, engrossing storyline to best use games as a new form of literature.

and give insight as Creative Director for *Darksiders* and 2012's *Darksiders II*. *Darksiders* is best described as a more mature *Legend of Zelda*. Players take control of War, one of the Four Horsemen of the Apocalypse, as he hunts down the source of an

Above Left:
Ultimate Alliance packaging

Above Right:
Batman: Rise of Sin Tzu art by Jim Lee

Above:
Darksiders II

end-of-the-world event initiated at the wrong time.

The quality of comic book-based video games made a significant leap with the release of *Batman: Arkham Asylum*, a game written by Batman guru Paul Dini, featuring the DC hero and his cast of foes, in 2009. The game sold over two million copies in its first three weeks of release—twenty times the number copies of *Detective Comics* sold in a typical month during 2009. The game went on to sell a total of 4.3 million copies and received extremely high marks from reviewers, earning the coveted Game of the Year award from the British Academy of Film and Television Arts and several video game magazines. Its 2011 sequel, *Batman: Arkham City*, expanded the cast to include Robin, Nightwing, and Catwoman as playable characters while placing the game within a free-roaming, *Grand Theft Auto*-style context. *Batman: Arkham City* sold two million copies in its first week of release, with the title on a trajectory to sell over six million copies. *Official PlayStation Magazine* called the game "[...] not only the best superhero game ever made, it's one of the best games ever made [...] it brings the Caped Crusader's world

to life better than any comic, movie, or television show before it." The magazine *Game Informer* gave *Arkham City* a perfect score, calling it "the best licensed video game ever made."

Enjoy the following interviews with comic book talents who delved into the video game industry. Some you will be absolutely familiar with, while others are names from the past that left the world of comics to pursue a career in video game production and design. I promise, however, that all of them will be insightful and entertaining as we look at tales from three decades of comic books and video games.

Left and Below:
Batman: Arkham Asylum game art

Above:
Batman: Arkham City game art

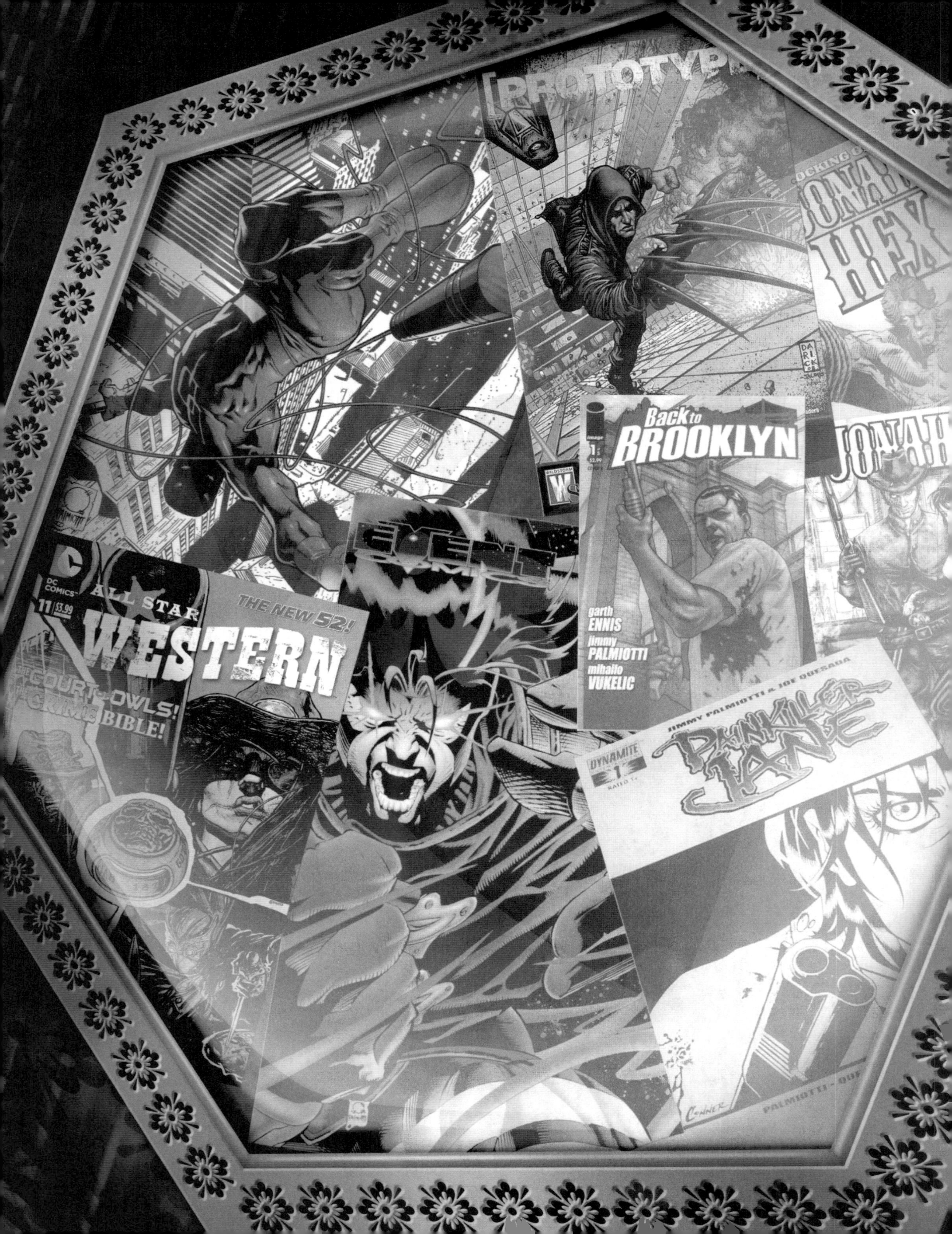
Back to BROOKLYN
image
$2.99
garth ENNIS
jimmy PALMIOTTI
mihailo VUKELIC
WILDSTORM
DC COMICS
11 $3.99
ALL STAR WESTERN
THE NEW 52!
BIBLE!
JIMMY PALMIOTTI & JOE QUESADA
PAINKILLER JANE
DYNAMITE
1

Jimmy**Palmiotti**

T wo-time Eisner nominee Jimmy Palmiotti made his mainstream comics debut in the Summer of 1991, inking *The 'Nam* and *Punisher* for Marvel Comics. Palmiotti was quickly paired with up-and-coming penciler, Joe Quesada, on the Valiant Comics titles *Ninjak* and *X-O Manowar*. This led to a successful partnership that saw Quesada and Palmiotti found Event Comics in 1994 and produce fan-favorite titles such as *Ash* and *Painkiller Jane*. Event Comics was contracted in 1998 by Marvel Comics to create the Marvel Knights line, headlined by a pairing of Palmiotti and Quesada with *Mallrats* director Kevin Smith for a classic *Daredevil* run.

In 2000, Jimmy Palmiotti began to add writing to his repertoire, starting with a successful stint on Marvel Comics' *Deadpool* and followed up with runs of *Jonah Hex*, *Hawkman*, and *Power Girl* from DC Comics. In 2002, Palmiotti, along with writing partner Justin Gray and penciler Amanda Connor, formed Paper Films, and through this company, Palmiotti has worked on a variety of video game related projects, beginning with *The Punisher* for the PlayStation 2 and Xbox. Palmiotti also performed a portion of the writing chores for the 2007 Sci-Fi Channel Original Series *Painkiller Jane*. In recent years, Palmiotti worked on the creator-owned series *Back to Brooklyn* for Image Comics as well as *All-Star Western* and *Unknown Soldier* for DC Comics' New 52 line.

Opposite: (clockwise)
Daredevil #1, Prototype #3, Jonah Hex #13, Jonah Hex #53, Painkiller Jane #1, Ash #1, All Star Western #10 and Back To Brooklyn #1

Above:
Ninjak

Keith Veronese: You have worked on a plethora of video game projects. How did you get started in video games? Was there an initial interest in the field?

Jimmy Palmiotti: I got started as a fluke. The first game I worked on was *The Punisher* (2005, developed by Volition, published by THQ). I got a call from my lawyer, Ken Levine, asking me if I could write video games, to which I replied, "Oh yeah, no sweat." Ken told me about Garth Ennis being offered the gig writing the game, but Garth had no experience doing this, and he didn't even play games other than *Pong* (1972, Atari). I spoke to Garth and we decided that, between the two of us, we could figure it out. The price tag on the gig made it even sweeter.

Once they approved us, I went to Amazon.com and ordered a few books on writing video games, and it went from there. Many times in my career I have just taken a job saying the same thing and then nailing it after a bit of research. Of all the games I worked on, [the execution of] that one came the closest to the work we had done for it.

Veronese: What is the writing process like for you? Is it any different when it comes to video games versus comic books or a screenplay?

Palmiotti: Yes, first, [writing video games] seems like it is never-ending because of all the levels and stages that come into the process of creating and then writing the game. In addition, unlike comics and screenwriting, you are usually working with at least a dozen people on all ends to get this huge undertaking under way. There is always some travel involved, because the game people want to show you off and meet you and have you in the room with them when they are pitching their ideas. I love that part of the process because I get to meet a lot of wonderfully creative people. Overall, [I would say] comics are the most simple, then screenplays, and

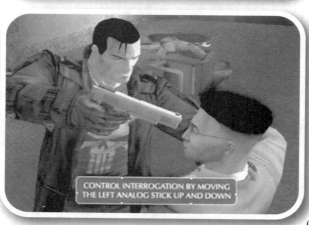

then video games.

Veronese: Did you work on the actual design document (an organizational document developed by a software designer to give the developmental team a guide with which to work) for *The Punisher*, *Ghost Rider* (2007, developed by Climax, published by 2K Games), or *Mortal Kombat vs. DC Universe* (2008, developed by Midway/Warner Brothers Interactive, published by Midway Games)? If so, how was this different from working off of a script for a comic book?

Palmiotti: I haven't worked on any design elements other than pitching the ideas for the locations, set pieces, and the overall look of the environments, but a lot of the game people did include us and did send us some sketches and ideas and Justin Gray and I gave our two cents.

That part of the process is long and involved, especially when dealing with a licensed property like the games we have worked on. I think the *Mortal Kombat* people had to go through at least a dozen rounds when designing the DC Universe characters to get them approved. That's a job with a million man hours attached to it.

Veronese: What would you say is the major difference between scripting for comics and scripting for video games? What would be some advantages and difficulties of each?

Palmiotti: Time and the approval process. With comics, we have been around (long) enough that an editor knows our work and reads the scripts looking for things we didn't see. We get notes, nail them, and the gig is done. With writing for games, we have budget restrictions, time restrictions, and multilayered documents that have to be written. Anyone that tells you game writing is

Above:
The Punisher package and screenshots of game

easy deserves a slap in the head. Now, the advantages and disadvantages other than time is that, in the end, they both pay around the same amount of money, believe it or not. If I clocked my total hours, it is around the same. The only good thing with games is if you can get royalties tied into your deal, you can wind up with a pretty nice paycheck. Oh, also, the perks.

The game people treat you like gold. They pay your way to events, all expenses, and fuss over you like crazy. Comic companies, well, they figure if you can't do something, they have got 100 other guys that will take your job. The comic business has gotten better lately, but unless you make a mark with distinctive work, you better have a second job.

Veronese: What is the typical length of a script for a video game?

Palmiotti: The last one I can remember working on was over 100 pages. [**Author's note**: *That is about three to four times the typical script for a monthly comic.*]

Veronese: As a writer, how do you prepare for the possibility of non-linear storylines in video games, a phenomenon not possible in mainstream comics?

Palmiotti: By playing and understanding the video game playing process. In my home I have an Xbox, a PlayStation 3, a Wii, and some portable systems. Like new comics, I go out and play each and every game I can. It's part of the job. Once you get it, you get it.

Veronese: What was the extent of your work on *Ghost Rider* and *The Punisher,* as they were movie tie-in games? Movie tie-in games aren't often known for their quality, however, THQ's *The Punisher* is thought of as one of the best tie-ins of all-time. Were there any challenges or preconceived notions that you brought to working on a movie tie-in?

Palmiotti: With both games, we understood that there were actual movies involved. I had to go

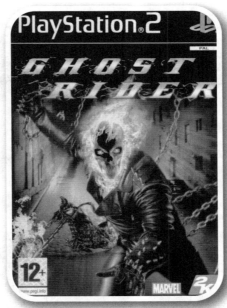

read the screenplays under locked door [with a] guard and take notes. I'm not kidding. The guys involved with THQ's *Punisher* game said "Go crazy." Garth Ennis and I got together over a few drinks and wrote a script that had a lot of elements from the comic book and a few of the movie that they fell in love with it. We got lucky on that one. On *Ghost Rider*, it started out okay, and then the game got sold to another company and then another and honestly, when we finally saw the finished game, we barely recognized it. It was a shame because some of the crazy things we created never made it into the game, but it was obvious this was a project that had a lot of re-boots involved each time it changed hands.

Veronese: Did you have any access to the video game *Dead Space* (2008, developed by EA Redwood Shores, published by Electronic Arts) while scripting *Dead Space: Downfall,* the animated prequel? This was a particularly strange situation as the prequel animated movie debuted simultaneously with the video game. What did you have to work off of for background material for the *Dead Space* universe?

Palmiotti: I went to EA Games headquarters in San Francisco with two people from Starz Media and sat with the *Dead Space* crew, the main designer, and writers. We got footage screened of the game and I got a set of designs to take with me for Justin Gray and I to use.

These designs included stuff like the interior of the ship so we would know how to script the screenplay and make it flow smoothly so both the game people and the film goers would get the same information. Our job was to create the complete backstory of why there was a mining

Above:
Ghost Rider package and screenshot

Left:
Dead Space packaging

ship in distress in outer space with monsters inside it. Justin and I had to create totally new characters, working alongside the EA Games and Starz Media people, and map out an outline that satisfied both clients. We had a decent amount of backstory but we really had to go in there, make sense of it, and make the existing backstory have a proper place in the film we were writing.

Veronese: Was it an unusual experience scripting a movie about a video game that was a new intellectual property and had not been released yet?

Palmiotti: Not only unusual, but exciting as hell since this was going to be our first screenplay that actually been made. We were pretty stoked. As usual, some scenes were changed and taken out that we wrote. For example, part of the final battle is a DVD extra on the disc, and we also had a pretty cool scene in wheat fields that was just too expensive to create.

Veronese: Did you have any input on the storyline for the original *Dead Space* video game?

Palmiotti: No, and that was fine. That was someone else's gig and I respect that.

Veronese: Did you have any involvement in the recently released, Wii exclusive *Dead Space: Extraction* (2009, developed by Visceral Games/Eurocom, published by Electronic Arts), which takes place during the period of *Dead Space: Downfall?*

Palmiotti: Unfortunately, the movie doing really well

Above: *Deadspace* stills

Below: *Mortal Kombat vs. DC Universe* stills

and being well received has nothing to do with us getting to work on the sequel (laughs). The game people changed hands [staying with publisher Electronic Arts, but changing developers from EA Redwood Shores to Visceral Games] and when that happens, people bring in their own people, which is a shame, but totally understood. We would have loved to be involved, but such is life. We are on to many other things these days.

Veronese: Are either of you working involved with the *Dead Space* live-action movie?

Palmiotti: Not at this moment, no, but we (Justin Gray and Jimmy Palmiotti) are involved in a couple of other films we can't talk about (right now). They should give us a call though. We can help.

Veronese: *Mortal Kombat vs. DC Universe* (2008, developed by Midway/Warner Brothers Interactive, published by Midway Games) presents some interesting challenges in that you get access to a whole new universe of characters, but at the same time, you have to pay homage to the legacy of each brand, as the *Mortal Kombat* franchise is known for excessive blood and gore while DC Comics/Warner Brothers would want to limit the extent of such violence. How and when did the job on *Mortal Kombat vs. DC Universe* come about? What was the extent of your work?

Palmiotti: John Nee (DC Senior Vice President of Business Development), asked if we could help out on the development of the game.

There were some problems between Midway and DC as far as the who and what of the characters. DC felt that having Justin and myself in there, in the mix, would help the process on both ends. We were hired as consultants, then got more involved with the story and levels, and then got the gig writing it with (Midway's) group. It was really exciting working side by side with Ed Boon (*Mortal Kombat* franchise co-creator) and his crew and the whole experience was a ton of fun.

Veronese: In regards to your work on *Prototype* (2009, developed by Radical, published by Activision), how does the experience change when your work is it to supply dialogue versus the whole story?

Palmiotti: We were writing the comic for Wildstorm off of the script (of the game) we were given. When the guys making the game read the comics, they thought we would be a good fit to write some of the background dialogue and such within the game. It's a big difference because what we were writing came after they had most of the main dialogue finished already, so our (input) was mostly police warnings, media interviews, and other background information that moved the story forward and gave a bit more story details away to the player while they were playing the game. It was an easy gig really because we were not creating any structure.

Veronese: Any plans to make a video game out of *Back to Brooklyn* (2008, Image Comics), especially since Garth Ennis (who co-wrote the Image Comics series with Palmiotti) and you both have experience writing video games? The series seems like a natural conversion to a video game.

Palmiotti: Well, we own the license with Kickstart Entertainment, and honestly, it is a natural for a shooter game. Nothing would make me happier to see this happen. As it is, Kickstart Entertainment is out there now selling the film rights, so you never know.

Veronese: Is there anything you've written into a video game (dialogue, violence, etc.) that was cut because it may influence a higher ERSB (Entertainment Software Rating Board) rating or because it

might compromise a property?

Palmiotti: Sure, but you don't worry about that. When we are writing, we come up with the wildest things possible and let (the ERSB) make those decisions. Each game had a scene or two cut and we are ok with that, but we always expect more (to be cut).

Veronese: Was there ever plans for an *Ash* (1994, Event Comics) video game?

Palmiotti: When DreamWorks bought the multimedia rights, Joe Quesada and I thought there would be a game once the film went into development. Five screenplays later, nothing happened, and they still have the rights. We are hoping someone realizes what they are sitting on, gets off their ass, and makes the film, so I can rightfully be involved with creating a game for it. That's Hollywood though—I am convinced they buy properties so others can't develop them.

Veronese: What has been your favorite experience while working in the video game field so far?

Palmiotti: Getting to work with extremely talented people, getting to go to E3 and have a blast at the Sony party with the Black Eyed Peas, and finally getting to sit down and play the games we all worked so hard to create.

Veronese: Do you see a future where the majority of your work takes place in the video game field?

Palmiotti: It would be nice, but I think of what I do as being a writer of all things: comics, games, and film. So, as for moving, exclusively for the video game, unless I create the character or game, I won't be there full-time.

Veronese: What is your video game system of choice and your top 3 games of all time?

Palmiotti: The PlayStation 3. I do have a real love for shooter games though. I love *Bejeweled* on my iPhone, but the top three are the *Call of Duty* series, the *Metal Gear Solid* series, and *The Punisher*.

Above:
Prototype game packaging

Left:
Ash #4 Ashcan cover: pencils by Joe Quesada with inks by Jimmy Palmiotti

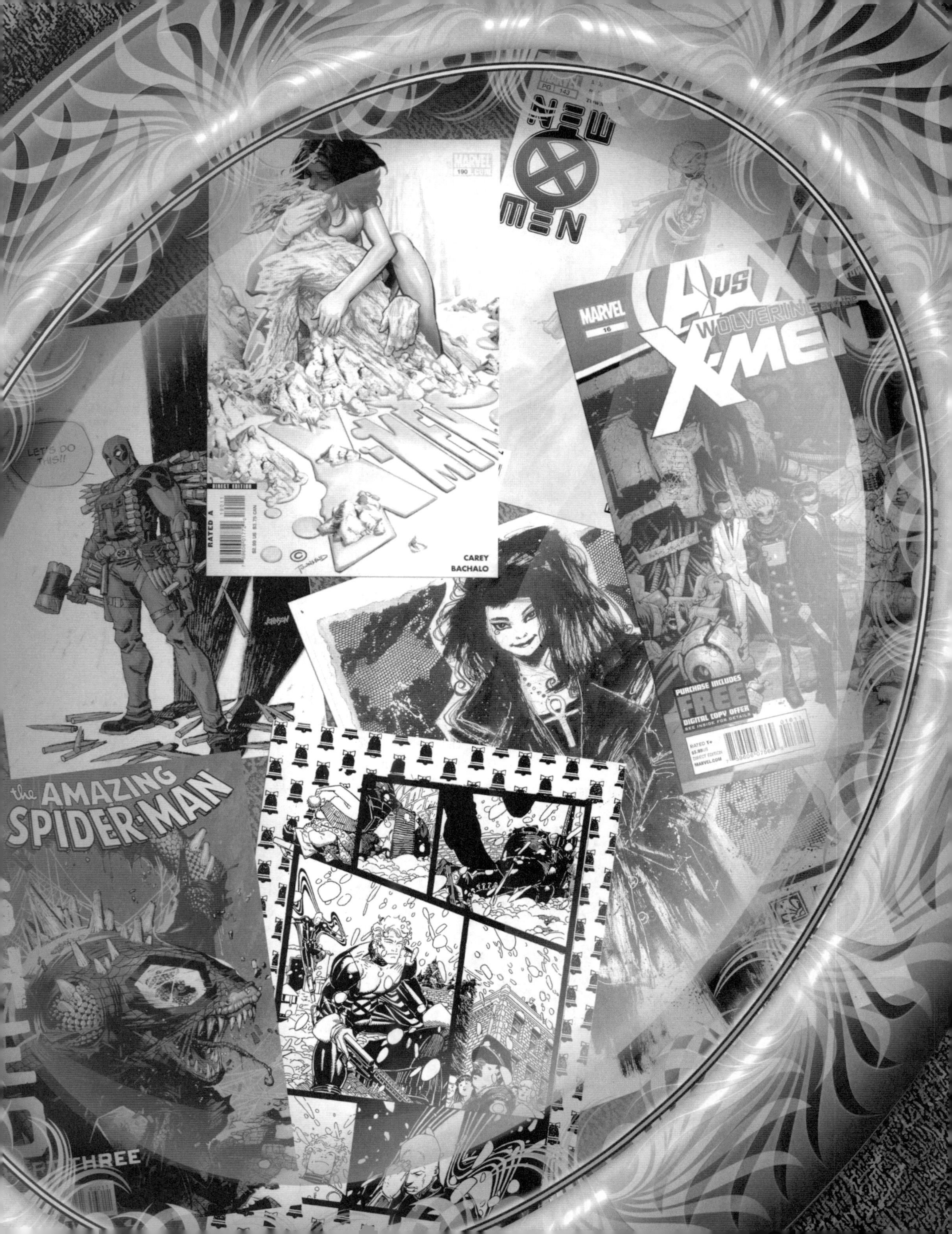
NEW X MEN
MARVEL
190
X-MEN
DIRECT EDITION
RATED A
CAREY
BACHALO
LET'S DO THIS!!
MARVEL
16
A VS X
WOLVERINE and the
X-MEN
PURCHASE INCLUDES
FREE
DIGITAL COPY OFFER
SEE INSIDE FOR DETAILS
MARVEL.COM
the AMAZING
SPIDER-MAN
THREE

Chris**Bachalo**

Chris Bachalo began his comic book penciling career in rarified air, with penciling chores on Neil Gaiman's *Sandman* as his first published work. Bachalo drew the now classic *Sandman* tie-ins *Death: The Time of Your Life* and *Death: The High Cost of Living* as well.

After finishing a stint at DC Comics, Bachalo moved on to Marvel, where he brought his unique style to *Generation X* as well as several other X-titles, including *Uncanny X-Men*, *Ultimate X-Men*, *New X-Men*, and mini-series that revisited the *Age of Apocalypse*. In the meantime, Bachalo also co-created *Steampunk* for Image Comics' Cliffhanger imprint. One can find Bachalo firmly working in the comic industry and bringing new work to shelves every month, but he has also worked on several video games, including *Army of Two: The 40th Day*.

Keith Veronese: How much interaction did you have with the team that worked on *Army of Two: The 40th Day*?

Chris Bachalo: Yeah, it was pretty simple, really. Matt Turner over at EA contacted me through my website about working on the project, and he turned me over to Creative Director Alex Hutchinson. They shared with me what the game was about and what they wanted me to do, and everything sounded reasonable enough and I jumped in. I had my choice of the good or bad morality cutscenes and I went for the good. One of the stories they shared with me involved a young boy and, as the parent of a young boy, I'm not emotionally equipped at this time to take on something bad involving a young one...

Veronese: Your work on *Army of Two: The 40th Day* centered on the role of "Morality Moments" in the game. Could you tell us a bit about these cut scenes?

Bachalo: As you play the game you'll run across characters, some of which you'll be asked to make an important morality decision about. For example, there's a scene in an embassy in which you encounter a guard. He's protecting the armory. Up pops

Opposite: (clockwise)
X-Men #190,
New X-Men #143,
Wolverine and
the X-Men #16,
Death Poster,
Generation X #4, The
Amazing Spider-Man
#632 and Deadpool #31

Above:
X-Men #200

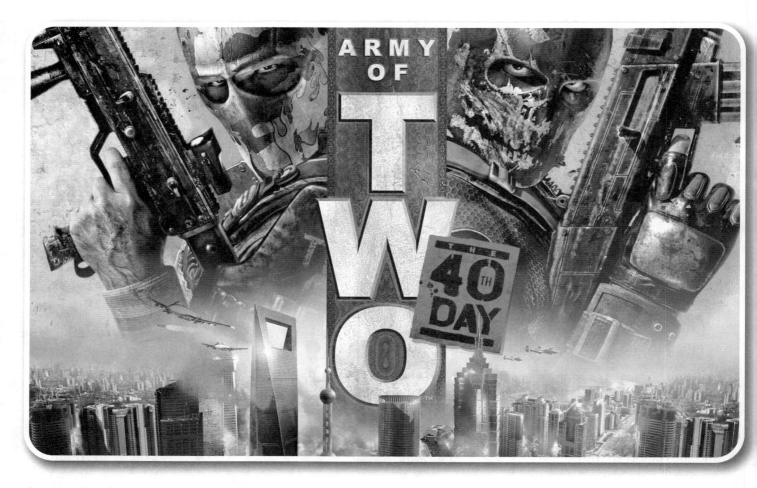

ARMY OF TWO

THE 40TH DAY

the morality button. You need to choose to let him live or to kill him. Once you've made your decision, the scene will continue, the guard will live or die as you've determined and then the morality flash forward will cut in. It'll show you in a series of illustrated images what happens to that person after you leave. It's a device designed to add a little more dimension to the supporting cast—to show that they are not simply obstacles designed to slow you down in the game—and to demonstrate that there are ramifications to one's actions. You know, like the rock thrown into the proverbial pond that creates a ripple effect. There are other lives being affected by your actions. More than just what is in front of you. Like in real life. If you run over a guy with your car, you not only hurt the guy, but the guy's family is affected and maybe the people that rely on him at work, etc.

When Matt and Alex started showing me the scripts they asked for input. This was great, because I'm full of ideas and shared with them the idea of perhaps making my positive morality cuts not so positive by adding shades of grey to the stories. They were curious and I shared with them ideas that I thought were really cool and let me run with them. I ended up creating a lot more work for myself as my

stories were longer than the 5 beat scenarios the game's writer had in mind, but it was worth it. I created stories that didn't always end well when you think you are doing the right thing, as in this case, letting the guard live. One of my favorite cuts involves a White Tiger. What do you do with a White Tiger that's interesting? You'll find out. It's great fun.

Veronese: Jock (*Scalped, Losers*) also worked on the game. Did you two have any interaction in creating the cut scenes?

Bachalo: They introduced the two of us via email and that was it. I'm a huge fan of his work and, as a result of previous experiences, I made a very conscious decision to avoid looking at what he was doing. At one point Alex asked if I wanted to see Jock's drawings, and I declined as I didn't want to be influenced by them. I had a pretty good train of thought as far as what I wanted the cuts to look like, and I know that if I saw what he was doing, I would get distracted. At one point near the end, I did see one pic and, after thinking, "Oh, wow!" because it was amazing, it was hard to stick with what I was doing. I just know that about myself. I suck up other influences like a sponge. Then I'm all screwed up...

Veronese: How was your experience different

than working in comics? Was there more freedom or less freedom than working off of a comic script?

Bachalo: I was expecting the worst. I figured, big corporation equals several hundred layers of bureaucracy. It ended up being quite the opposite. Using the script as an example, Alex asked for ideas, welcomed them and then let me roll. All the best creative/art directors work that way. They know the talent, hire them and then let them do their thing. When I turned the stories in, I scribbled up thumbnails of the story beats, and, once approved, set to work on the finals, turned those in, and moved on to the next level. There was never anything like getting this guy's approval or that guy's approval. Alex was the one making the yes or no decisions, which is the best. Occasionally, there were few items that needed to be adjusted, but it was never anything nitpicky or Earthmoving. Creatively, it was a great experience, and I ended up writing all my own stories, which was even better. This is very similar to my current creative freedom in comics. Once the script is handed over to me, I pretty much have the green go to move onto final art. It is something that I've been doing for awhile and I've earned the editors' confidence that I'll make the right decisions with the story.

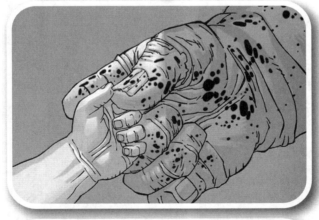

Opposite:
Army of Two: The 40th Day promotional art

Above & Below:
Army of Two: The 40th Day game art

Veronese: Is there any other video game work in your immediate future?

Bachalo: I worked on a Nintendo DS game about two years ago that has not been released, but, other than that, I don't have anything lined up...

Veronese: Are you a video game player? Any favorite games?

Bachalo: I'm not. This will sound a little weird, but I learned a while back that I'm not a good finger person, that I'm a good hand/arm person. What the heck does that mean? It means that I'm really lousy with things involving fingers, like guitar, piano, keyboards, and pushing buttons on video game controllers. I'm all thumbs with those things. Slowest, dumbest typist you've ever seen. I'm good with hand/arm things: hockey sticks, baseball bats, throwing balls, most tools, and pushing a pencil across paper. So, as much as I would like to play the games I found that I really suck because I'm always pushing the wrong buttons. That and I'm burnt out at the end of the day, and the idea of dealing with the stress of not getting killed in a video game is too much. I'll relax watching an hour or two of *The Shield* or something like that before calling it a day. I do play *Need For Speed* with my son. We bought two steering wheel consoles and we race. I'm pretty good at that—no buttons.

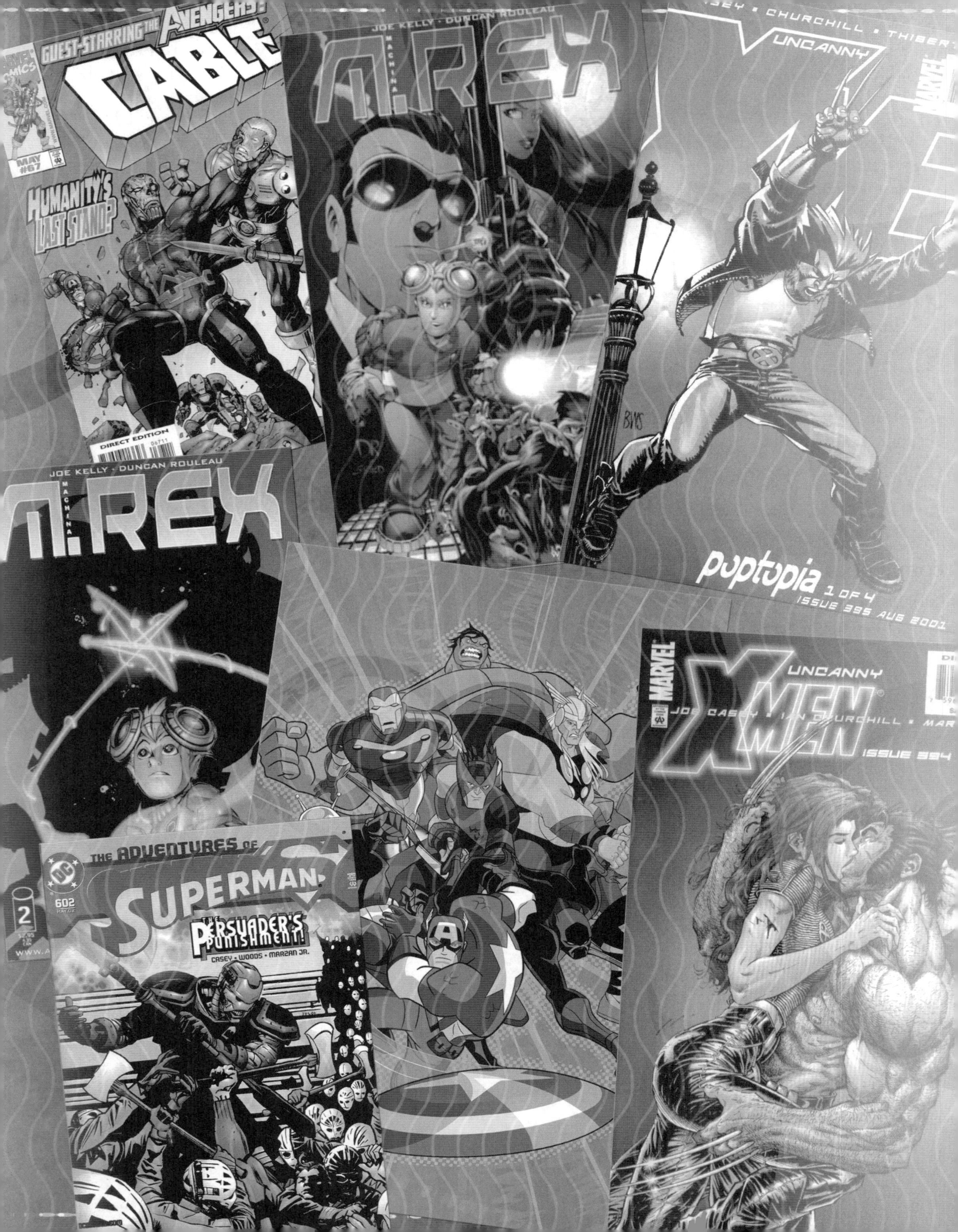
GUEST-STARRING THE AVENGERS!
CABLE
MARVEL COMICS
MAY #67
HUMANITY'S LAST STAND?
DIRECT EDITION
JOE KELLY · DUNCAN ROULEAU
MACHINA
M.REX
CHURCHILL • THIBER
UNCANNY
poptopia 1 OF 4
ISSUE 395 AUG 2001
JOE KELLY · DUNCAN ROULEAU
MACHINA
M.REX
MARVEL
UNCANNY
X-MEN
ISSUE 394
THE ADVENTURES OF
SUPERMAN
602
THE PERSUADER'S PUNISHMENT!
CASEY • WOODS • MARZAN JR.

Joe**Casey**

Joe Casey first received critical acclaim for his alternative take on Marvel tough guy/super mutant Cable, teaming up for French artist Ladronn for an amazing run. Casey followed up this successful and entertaining run with a stint on G.I. Joe for Devil's Due

Press along with writing *Wildcats*, *Adventures of Superman*, and *Uncanny X-Men*.

Casey, along with fellow comic book veterans Joe Kelly, Duncan Rouleau, and Steven T. Seagle formed Man of Action, a studio/think tank for multi-media properties that spawned the successful cartoon franchises *Ben 10* and *Generation Rex*. As a part of Man of Action, Casey also writes for the *Ultimate Spider-Man* and *Avengers: Earth's Mightiest Heroes* cartoon series.

Keith Veronese: Prior to *X-Men Legends*, you wrote *Cable* for two years, taking the character in a decidedly different, but fan-enjoyed direction (and one that is still maintained by Marvel continuity) and spent a year and a half writing *Uncanny X-Men*. How were you approached to work on *X-Men Legends*?

Joe Casey: They approached me strictly because I was writing *Uncanny X-Men* at the time. It was a case of asking, "Are you interested?" At first, I wasn't interested, but the more I thought about it, the more I realized I could pull in the entire Man of Action team (which was a relatively new company at the time) and we could gang-write the game. It was a high-profile gig in a

Opposite: (clockwise)
Cable #67, M. Rex #1, Uncanny X-Men #395, Uncanny X-Men #394, The Avengers Earths Mightiest Heroes, The Adventures of Superman #602, and M. Rex #2

Above:
Ben 10

huge media space that existed outside of comics and, at that moment, really gave our company some legitimacy.

Veronese: Were you given any story direction for *X-Men Legends*?

Casey: Not that I can recall. I do remember that, at first, it was going to reflect more of the then current *Ultimate X-Men* continuity, since that was the hot X-Men property at the time. I also remember a few character texts where they were wearing the Frank Quitely-designed rescue uniforms from the *New X-Men* book. Eventually, they settled on a basic, all-purpose version of the characters. Story-wise, we traveled to Madison, Wisconsin where Raven Software, the developers of *X-Men Legends*, were located. We broke the story in the room, basically. As it turns out, what we came up with—and ultimately wrote—was way bigger than what they were able to do.

Veronese: What specific parts did you work on and what roles did you play in writing the game?

Casey: Once we had the story approved, we broke it up into acts. As I recall, I wrote Act One, which basically served to set up the storyline for the game. The workload was pretty evenly split, and it was some of the most difficult writing I've ever done.

Veronese: About how long were you involved with the *X-Men Legends* project?

Casey: It was a while ago, so it's tough to remember exactly how long we were in the trenches. Probably about two years from beginning to end, but that was sporadic writing over that period of time.

Veronese: How was working on a video game different from working on a comic book versus a cartoon series?

Casey: Writing for video games is its own unique beast. There are elements of it—the cinematics, for example—that are similar to

straight up screenwriting. But a task like writing incidental character dialogue that you might hear during gameplay is something you simply don't do in any other medium.

Veronese: Have you directly worked on any of the *Ben 10* games or the upcoming *Generator Rex* game?

Casey: They run those things by us in a very generalized way, but we're way too busy to get too involved in the ancillary material when it comes to those shows. Frankly, we're too occupied creating new concepts and selling new shows!

Veronese: How did Joe Kelley, Joe Kelly, Duncan

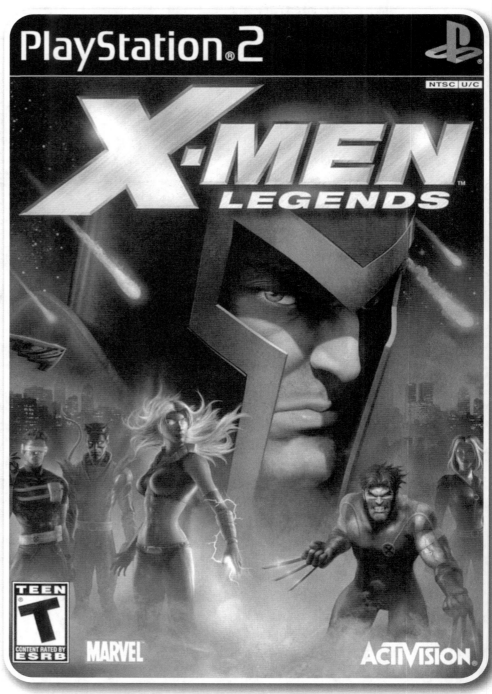

Rouleau, Steven Seagle, and yourself come about to form Man of Action?

Casey: I'm really tempted to say... we were visited by a man on a flaming pie. Actually, I might let that statement stand. I'm sure one of the other MoA partners will have a more straightforward answer.

Veronese: What projects do you work on that come under the MoA umbrella? What portion of your time is spent on Man of Action-related projects?

Casey: These days, most everything we do is related to Man of Action. It's our primary business. Creator-owned comics, animated series, television shows, feature films... it's all under the MoA bullet. We strive to be the model entertainment factory of the 21st Century.

Veronese: You say your work on *X-Men Legends* was some of the most difficult writing you've ever done—what were some of the hurdles to overcome?

Casey: Video game writing isn't just writing pure, linear stories. All the different levels, the side quests, etc.—it's just a different form for a writer to have to wrap your mind around. It wasn't something that came naturally to me, in particular. I'm just glad the game turned out okay.

Veronese: How did you all divide up the work on *X-Men Legends*? Was it completely separate, or would you grab a draft of something of Kelley's and run with it, or vice versa?

Casey: After we broke the story, like I said, we each took separate "acts" of the story and started writing. I never really saw what the other guys were writing until way after the fact. I had my hands full with my act. I don't recall if one of us did a clean-up pass on the whole thing. God, I can't imagine who took that on. Wasn't me, I can tell you that.

Veronese: What prompted the four of you to start Man of Action?

Casey: It was all about the simple concept of strength in numbers. We thought, as pop culture was turning more toward comic books—and comic book

creators—as source material, we wanted to be ready. Turns out we were ahead of the curve after all.

Veronese: Are there any other Man of Action properties that you think would fit particularly well as a video game or any other Man of Action properties that have video games in the works?

Casey: More than a few, I'm sure. We've even created a few specific video game concepts. Quite a few years ago, we dreamed up a role-playing game called *ATOM X*, where the player would receive superpowers but were able to choose within the game whether or not you're going to be a superhero or a super-villain. Based on your choice, the world of the game, the other characters within it, would react accordingly.

Veronese: Do you play video games? If so, are you a console or PC gamer? Do you have any favorites?

Casey: Honestly, I crossed a personal line in the sand a few years ago... where I play fewer games, read fewer comics, and watch fewer movies and less television. It is probably because it's my job to *make* those things, so I have a lot less time to enjoy them as a fan. Luckily, the buzz I get from pure creation cannot be matched by consuming media.

Veronese: What's a typical work day for you like? Do you typically stick with a single project or move between projects? Is Man of Action a studio in the figurative sense, or are you all working together under one roof?

Casey: This is the 21st Century... virtual studios are where it's at. As far as what makes up a "typical" work day? There ain't no such thing. There's so much stuff to do, so many projects in various stages of development, every day is a new set of challenges. It's the best way to work, really, because you're never bored.

Opposite:
X-Men Legends packaging

Above:
X-Men Legends scree shot

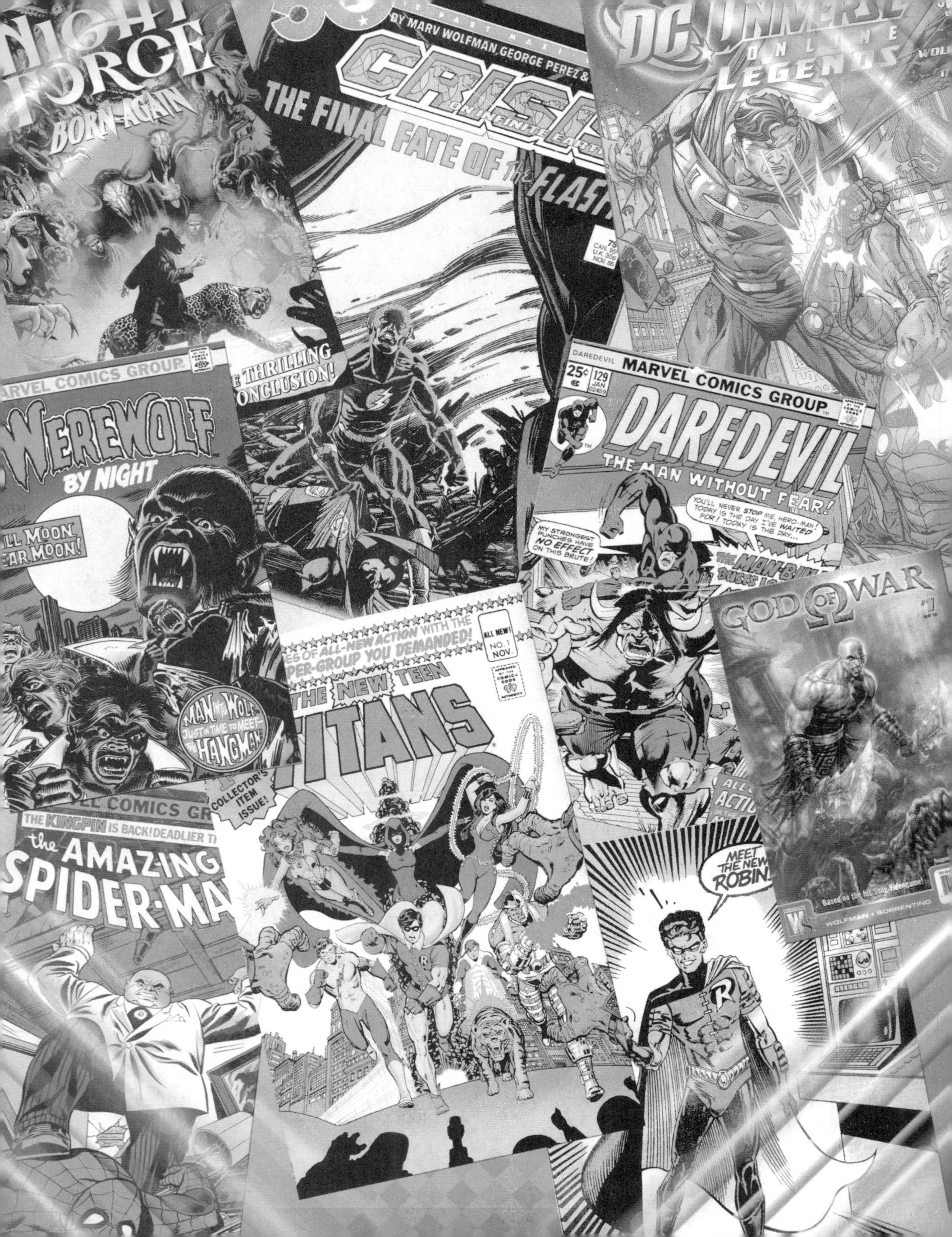

BORN AGAIN
BY MARV WOLFMAN, GEORGE PEREZ &
CRISIS ON INFINITE EARTHS
THE FINAL FATE OF the FLASH
DC UNIVERSE ONLINE LEGENDS
THE THRILLING CONCLUSION!
MARVEL COMICS GROUP
WEREWOLF BY NIGHT
MAN INTO WOLF — JUST IN TIME TO MEET — THE HANGMAN!
DAREDEVIL
25¢ 129 JAN
MARVEL COMICS GROUP
DAREDEVIL
THE MAN WITHOUT FEAR!
YOU'LL NEVER STOP ME, HERO-MAN! TODAY IS THE DAY I'VE WAITED FOR! TODAY IS THE DAY...
MY STRONGEST PUNCHES HAVE NO EFFECT ON THIS BRUTE!
GOD OF WAR
#1
ALL NEW! NO. 1 NOV.
SUPER-GROUP YOU DEMANDED!
THE NEW TEEN TITANS
COLLECTOR'S ITEM ISSUE!
THE KINGPIN IS BACK! DEADLIER TH
the AMAZING SPIDER-MA
MEET THE NEW ROBIN!
Based on the hit Sony Videogame!
WOLFMAN • SORRENTINO

Marv**Wolfman**

Marv Wolfman created comic book superstar Blade with legendary artist Gene Colan for Marvel Comics while penning *Tomb of Dracula*. Wolfman is well known and esteemed for his successful efforts to ensure that comic book writers are given credit in print for the stories they write.

In 1980, Wolfman launched *New Teen Titans* with George Pérez, and the duo continued their working relationship on the epic continuity-changing crossover *Crisis on Infinite Earths*, a series that still undulates throughout the DC Universe. While at DC, Wolfman also created Tim Drake, the third character to don the Robin mantle.

Keith Veronese: What was your first video game work and how did you did the job come about?

Marv Wolfman: It's hard to say. Back in the 1980s, I wrote the *Captain Power* videotape games. After that I also did some work on a video game/ride for Disney Imagineering in the 1990s. More recently I co-wrote the dialogue for *Superman Returns* with Flint Dille. Flint is one of, if not the top, video game writers in the field and I was brought in as the Superman guy and Flint as the video game guy. That game may not have worked out exactly as everyone hoped for, but Flint very kindly taught me about video game writing. I had known Flint ever since we were co-story editors on the original *Transformers* cartoon show. Since then I went on to write a number of other games.

Veronese: What was your role on the *Captain Power* videotape games—was it a mixture of teleplay and game scenarios?

Wolfman: The game was one of target shooting, but we needed a slight narrative to keep it going. I wrote a full script to set up the story.

Veronese: What were some of the non-video game related games you worked on?

Wolfman: I think the Disney Dinosaur-raft ride—which in some form is at DisneyQuest in Orlando, would be the biggest one.

Veronese: How did you become involved with *DC Universe Online*? How long have you been involved and what has been your role?

Opposite: (clockwise)
Night Force #7, Crisis on Infinite Earths #8, DC Universe Online Legends #13, Daredevil #129, God of War #1, Robin, The New Teen Titans #1, The Amazing Spider-Man #197, and Werewolf By Night #11

Above:
Tomb of Dracula #10

Wolfman: Boring answer: I was asked to join the project and said yes. How could I not? The game has got to be one of the best anywhere and to be even a small part of it is wonderful. My role has been to help them create an endless number of DC Comics-oriented missions. These missions exist so that the adventures the player goes out on are the kinds that will fit with the heroes or villains they may be working alongside. There was a mandate our direction had to be 100% DC-centric and, working along with Jim Lee, Geoff Johns, and a few other DC people, I worked to that end. I have been on the *DC Universe Online* project almost 2 years at this point.

Veronese: Do you play video games or have you played them in the past?

Wolfman: I've been playing video games ever since *Pong.* I had a Coleco-Vision console in the old days, then moved onto PC games then to the PS2, PS3, XBox 360, and the Wii, all of which I own and play on regularly.

Veronese: As a video game player, is there anything in the realm of current video game storytelling that frustrates you or you think could be vastly improved on?

Wolfman: I love straightforward first-person shooter games, but even my favorites are very much games where the player can only follow the path the designers set out for them, so my experience is pretty much the same as the next player and the player after them, with only minor variations. I would love to see these kind of story-driven games become more player controlled; where the events don't always play out the same way each time, and where the player affects more of the outcome of the game, can move off course, but still not be totally open world. We do

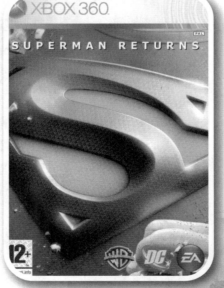

Above: (l to r)
Captain Power game packaging
Captain Power advertisement

Above: (l to r)
Superman Returns packaging
Superman Returns game art

Opposite: (top to bottom)
DC Universe Online promotional art

have these kinds of games, but I would love to see us move even more in that direction. At the same time, of course, I love that people are doing very different kinds of games, that the industry is still very much open to experimentation. I do like story games, but I also like *Portal* and *Angry Birds* and things between. I don't want all games to be the same.

Veronese: Do you have any favorite games at the moment?

Wolfman: Every week my friend Scott, who lives in Tennessee, and I play Ops missions from *Modern Warfare 2* online. We're down to the final 2 just in time for the new *Call of Duty*. I'm still playing *God of War 3* (I took time off while I was writing the *God of War* mini-series for Wildstorm so as not to have *God of War* overkill) but I am stuck at, I think it is Chronos; I'm climbing an arm but can't figure out what I do next. But man, that game is fun. Hopefully I will be done before this sees print. I think I'm going to start *StarCraft 2* soon as well as *World of Warcraft: Cataclysm*, which sounds like a good jumping on point for someone who hasn't played it for a while. And, of course, I'm waiting with baited breath for *DC Universe Online* to officially come out so I can play that through. Having a

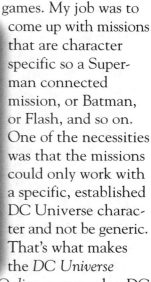

Mac I couldn't play the Beta except when I was in Austin. But I'll play the real version on my PS3.

Veronese: With *DC Universe Online*, are you in more of a plotting and scripting role? How would plotting/scripting for a video game be different from that on a comic book? Does it appear to change once the game has been published, but content is still being created?

Wolfman: In MMOs you don't really do scripting in the way you would with comics or even console games. My job was to come up with missions that are character specific so a Superman connected mission, or Batman, or Flash, and so on. One of the necessities was that the missions could only work with a specific, established DC Universe character and not be generic. That's what makes the *DC Universe Online* very much a DC game instead of a game about characters you know nothing about. Although the missions are original, they feel like you could have seen them in the comics.

I don't quite understand, but MMOs put the tools in the players hand and they decide how to deal with the missions, which missions to take, and even how much of it they want to do. In straightforward fiction the writer typically makes all those decisions.

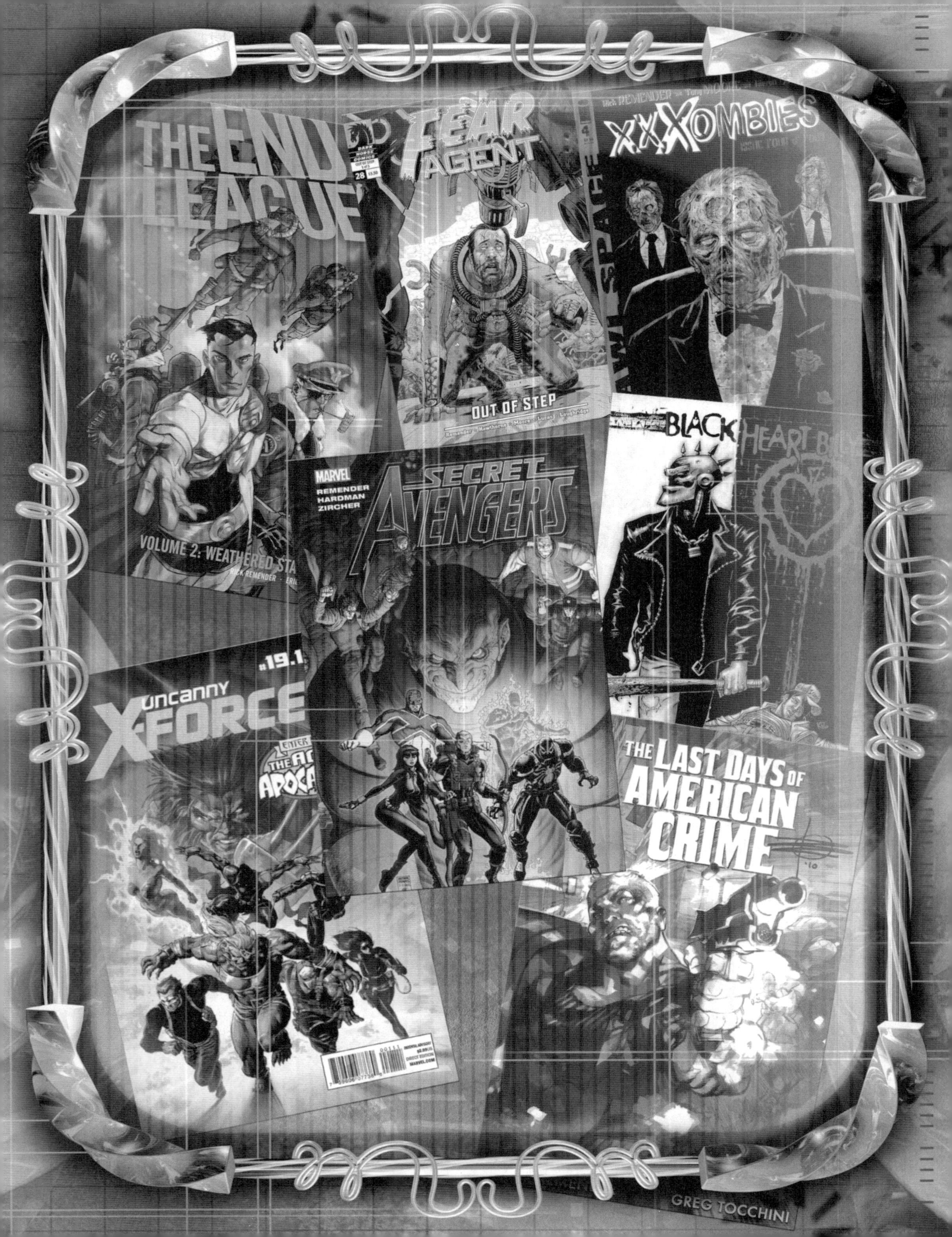
THE END LEAGUE
DARK HORSE COMICS
28
FEAR AGENT
OUT OF STEP
Remender · Hawthorne · Moore · Lucas · Loughridge
XXXOMBIES
VOLUME 2: WEATHERED STA
RICK REMENDER
MARVEL
REMENDER
HARDMAN
ZIRCHER
SECRET AVENGERS
BLACK
#19.1
UNCANNY
X-FORCE
THE LAST DAYS OF
AMERICAN
CRIME
GREG TOCCHINI

Rick**Remender**

Rick Remender worked for several years in the animation industry, helping create films like *Titan A.E.* and *The Iron Giant* before moving on back to the world of comics. His pride and joy is the creator-owned *Fear Agent*, a thirty-two issue sci-fi series that tells the story of Heath Huston as he tries to reunite his family amidst battles with alcoholism and intergalactic invaders.

Remender is probably best known for his amazing run on *Uncanny X-Force*, a series that brought many "lost" comic book fans to the world of monthly comics. Remender took readers back to the world of the Age of Apocalypse through the "Dark Angel Saga" and developed the backstory for fan-favorite X-character, Fantomex. Remender's work in a variety of media made him a natural to write and form the world of *Bulletstorm*, released by Epic Games for the Xbox 360 and PS3.

Keith Veronese: Electronic Arts appears to be making a dedicated effort to seek out known comic book talent for production work in their games (Chris Bachalo and Jock on *Army of Two: The 40th Day*, Palmiotti on *Dead Space: Downfall*). How were you approached by Electronic Arts to work on *Dead Space*?

Rick Remender: The work on *Dead Space* came about a result of some story-board work I did at Electronic Arts on the *007: From Russia with Love* James Bond franchise. On that project I worked with Cate (Latchford), Glen (Schofield), and Chuck (Beaver), the producers of *Dead Space*. Some of the comics I was writing at the time like *Fear Agent* were circulating in the Electronic Arts offices. When they started moving forward on *Dead Space*, they brought me in as one of the writers

RICK REM3ND3R · PAUL R3NAUD

DƎVOLUTION

Opposite: (clockwise)
The End League Volume II TPB, *Fear Agent* #28, *XXXombies* #4, *Black Heart Bully* promotional art, *The Last Days of American Crime* #2, *Uncanny X-Force* #19.1, and *Secret Avengers* #22

Above:
Devolution promotional art

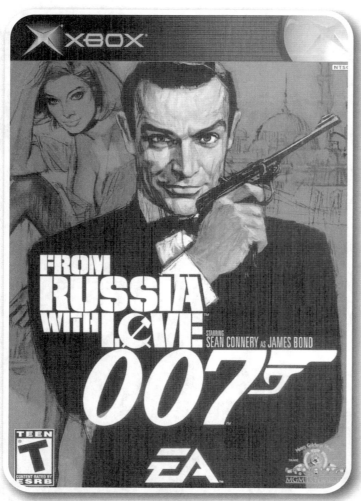

me bastardize an impression of him.

Veronese: I'm sure he gets that all the time. So you started working on *Dead Space* around the early issues of *Fear Agent*, so issues four and five would have been circulating around the Electronic Arts offices?

Remender: At least the first two *Fear Agent* trades were out at that point. I started sometime around 2007.

Veronese: What was your official position on *Dead Space*? Were you working with a team of writers?

Remender: Yes—Warren Ellis did a lot of the foundation work and then they had me come in and do the first four or five drafts of the full script, building up a lot of different scenarios. I moved back to Portland during that time and I went back to EA Redwood a couple of times to work with them and flesh out some of the ideas they had and smooth out some of the kinks. After that, I took the beats and wrote them into scenes.

for the game.

Veronese: *007: From Russia with Love* was the Sean Connery version, where EA went back and made Connery the star of the series, right? That was a great game.

Remender: That's the one. When we were doing the animatics for *007: From Russia with Love*, we were recording scratch tracks to go over the animatics for Connery to listen to while watching the sequences. They asked me to record the audio for these because I did the very worst Sean Connery impression. Basically, it was the *Saturday Night Live* "You win this one, Trebek!" version. It was a lot of fun to know that Sean Connery was getting to listen to me doing a terrible impression of him while he was doing the dialogue for the game.

Veronese: And he's sitting on the other side of the world in some Italian Villa…

Remender: Hearing

Above
007: From Russia With Love packaging

Right:
007: From Russia With Love game art

Opposite:
Dead Space game art

Veronese: Did you do any dialogue work?

Remender: I did not. My job was to write a fifty- to sixty-page document that took the outline, which was two or three pages of beats, and expand it into an actual treatment that was the next step toward creating a script. There was some rough dialogue in there, but, for the most part, all of the dialogue was by Antony Johnston, who did the final pass.

Veronese: *Dead Space* was a very popular game, and one of the best selling new intellectual properties in gaming in the past couple of years.

What can you tell us about *Bulletstorm*? It is a particularly interesting case, since it is one of the first video games to directly promote the fact that a comic book writer is on board with the project.

Remender: When Electronic Arts brought me on board, there were some very basic building blocks in place. I went to Poland, where (the video game developer) People Can Fly is located, and spent eight days with Adrian (Chmielarz), Tanya (Jessen), and the rest of the *Bulletstorm* team there, and pitched a lot of different ideas—the "space pirate" angle and a bunch of different things. Then we took them and workshopped it for seven or eight days until we had a nice pass at the story that also contained some of the

landmarks they needed to meet for the video game. Adrian, the creative director and game designer, is a fan of two of my books, *Fear Agent* and *Black Heart Billy*, and tonally I wanted to lean into the pulp science-fiction aspect, but to go much, much further into the B-movie schlock talk that I did in *Black Heart Billy*, where I let myself be unhindered in my joy of writing perversion and filth. Given that the characters in *Bulletstorm* are space pirates and former military, it seemed to fit. Everyone responded well to it, and I like to write humor that is sort of doused in twelve-year-olds' glee of using profanity. That stuck and became a part of the tone of the game.

Veronese: You can certainly see that humor come out in the demo videos for *Bulletstorm* that have been circulated prior to its release. In a way, it almost feels like it is a *Fear Agent* game, but with the humor taken to an extreme level.

Remender: The pulp sci-fi elements are obviously going to have some similarities with what we do in *Fear Agent*. But where as *Fear Agent* is sort of a human drama, where you are dealing with an alcoholic who is a torn-up, broken down man and drawing you into a character story, these characters (in *Bulletstorm*) are not as redeemable, and the tone is much more over the top and anything can go.

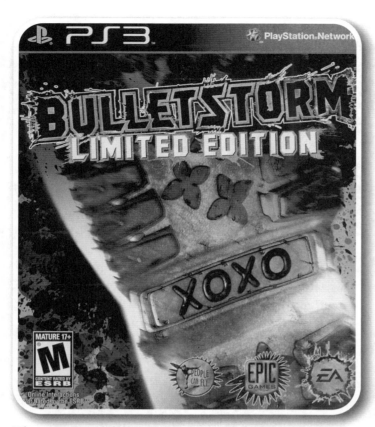

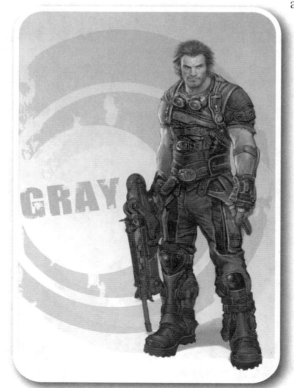

That is sort of the joy of pulp science-fiction—it's more about the imagination and the set pieces than explaining how they came about.

Veronese: You kind of step back in *Fear Agent* every once in a while and there is this introspective look that you are able to do in comics that you might not be able to do in video games.

Remender: But there is a real human side of *Bulletstorm* and all of the insanity is kind of explained. You basically have crashed on this Dubai-style vacation world where all the radiation filters broke. All of the natural life of the planet and the people who couldn't evacuate become mutated. So it's sort of *Road Warrior* meets *The Toxic Avenger* in a super-future Dubai. The set-up, in terms of the science-fiction aspect, is not about trying to make sense of the radiation and how it turns things into giant Godzilla-esque monsters. It's just about understanding that radiation makes these things

happen.

Veronese: That's one thing I really enjoy about your writing style. In *Fear Agent*, you don't explain how a wormhole is created, it just pops up in the story and it exists, without wasting two pages of the issue explaining why or how the wormhole exists. The wormhole is there, and you've created an environment where the reader believes the characters have the technology, and you move the story along.

Remender: Hopefully there are some rules to reality though where there is not a *deus ex machina* every few panels where they are like, "And now I have a time jump device." The necessary materials are still difficult to obtain, but I don't get into the scientific details of how the warp drive works, it's more of like, "Now we have super fuel and we used it to go back into time," and you are like, ok, we are on an adventure.

Veronese: It seems like a lot of modern comics and media is trending toward a "hard" sci-fi edge, with an explanation for everything works.

Remender: And I'm just not interested in that. I want to be grounded in character more than I want to be grounded in the world the character is in.

Veronese: Do you play any video games? What are you playing right now?

Remender: I play a lot of *Call of Duty* with friends and I've got a buddy who comes over a lot and we play *Street Fighter*. We've had a *Street Fighter* competition going on

Top Left:
Bulletstorm game packaging

Above, Left & Opposite:
Bulletstorm concept art

for years wherein he is Ken and I am E. Honda, constantly battling it out and looking for new ways to beat each other. But yeah, I play a lot of games— *Skate*, *Guitar Hero*, *Assassin's Creed*, *God of War*, and *Grand Theft Auto*. A lot of games.

Veronese: So you're obviously a gamer. I have heard a lot of comic writers use online gaming, playing games like *Halo* or *Call of Duty*, to talk to fellow writers and flesh out ideas.

Remender: I have never used it to flesh out storylines, but I play with other writers and talk shop for some faux social time.

Veronese: Have you played an early build of *Bulletstorm*?

Remender: I have not. I've seen it though and it is pretty terrific. Beyond being not only excited to see something you've written come to life and become playable, which is tremendous, there is also a fear that when the game comes out you won't dare to play it, and that's definitely not the case. I'm eager to get my hands on it and use the game engine to start whipping and grabbing guys and throwing them around and really leaning into the cartoon violence.

BULLETSTORM
Flytrap boss

Veronese: It will be really nice to have a first-person shooter with an emphasis on story content as well.

Remender: I think it's nice when something lets you know it doesn't take itself seriously and allows you to fall into the characters and realize you really do care about them. A lot of people mistake melodrama or seriousness for weight and gravity, especially in gaming. There seems to be a population that thinks that if a game doesn't take itself seriously, it cannot be good. To me, that's the opposite of what is true. The things I love always take themselves lightly, but then give me a lot in the way of character building and story. That is what I've tried to bring to *Bulletstorm*; you're playing the game, laughing and there are space pirates all around and they are fighting and crashing, and then, an hour into the game, you find yourself very invested in seeing the characters accomplish their goals and hopefully get what they want. That's not like a situation in gaming where something is forced down your throat, like something in the story where the world is about to face Armageddon if the player's character cannot get to the launch site in Russia. That's melodrama.

Veronese: And melodrama is easy.

Remender: It is way easier. Writing comedy that also has heart, writing something that is funny but is still "in character," that sort of thing takes way longer to do. You have to get the cadence of the dialogue bouncing, to find a way to have a pirate swearing where it is not all "f*ck this and f*ck that," but something that might actually make the player chuckle or think the character is clever. That is where the tone of *Bulletstorm* is and that is where I have spent a lot of my time, tweaking dialogue and placing a nice bit of comic relief in tense situations. I want the characters to entertain you while you play, so you are hearing chatter that isn't just exposition. Chatter that entertains the player and keeps them immersed in the story instead of something like, "Hey, we need to get up there and blow up that bridge," and getting from Point A to Point B.

Veronese: That's certainly something necessary in order for video games to evolve as an art and intellectually.

Remender: Mostly. The idea is something along the idea of the intellectual masked in the juvenile.

Veronese: Video games are almost as much a shared experience as books now. My friends and I are much more likely to discuss the storyline of an open-ended, character-driven game than something on television or a book.

Veronese: Did you have any interaction with Cliff Bleszinski (*Unreal Tournament*, the *Gears of War* series), one of the "stars" of our generation of gaming, while working on *Bulletstorm*?

Remender: Quite a bit. Cliff would be in on the story reviews and give comments and ideas, but in a really nice manner. A lot of times when you are starting a job on a game like this where there is so much on the line, you will get people that make it impossible to relinquish control and let you work. The really great work comes when I am not thinking about what my bosses want, but what I want, and what is coming purely from a creative place where what I am focused on is just the intention, immersing myself in whatever that intention may be. A lot of the time when you have too many strings on the puppet and people are pulling you in different directions, it can throw you off a bit. The producers of *Bulletstorm* were really great in that they stood way back and just told us to go nuts. That went for the creation of the world and the cast of characters. They wanted a cyborg involved, but they were fine with however we inserted the character in. Some of the elements they wanted were classic tropes which are fun to play with anyway, but in terms of Epic's involvement with Cliff and Tanya, it was pain free. Occasionally Cliff would have a note or an idea, but it wasn't pushed down your throat or heavy handed. It was just a, "Hey consider that we might want to do this here or that we might want to tweak things here." A lot of times the direction was great and really helped out in the production.

Veronese: Bleszinski's track record shows he certainly knows what he's doing.

Veronese: Would some of this freedom be a part of being lead writer on a project instead of staff writer?

Remender: Yes. On *Dead Space* I didn't really get to define or set the tone of the story and the characters and the world were already in place. It was a writing job. The character was in the mess hall in beat one, and in beat two he finds the captain's room and the captain turns into a monster. Those beats are provided for you and it is just a matter of fleshing out how things work and determining the best way to stage events. One is fleshing out, while the other is creating and fleshing out. Being involved in both lets me become heavily invested.

Veronese: You have a significant background in animation (*Iron Giant, Titan A.E.*) and comic art work as well (inking on *Avengers*).

Remender: The inking on *Avengers* is the least of the artwork I've done, but unfortunately it's a big Marvel book and a lot of people have seen it. It is something I became known for in the middle of my career and it has been a kind of pain in the ass to unburden myself of the perception of being "the guy who inked *Avengers*." I've penciled five graphic novels worth of material and unfortunately inked one or two graphic novels worth of material that a lot of people saw.

Veronese: Was your background in animation beneficial in beginning your video game work,

Above:
Bulletstorm concept art

especially in light of working on projects involving a large number of departments and people or giving a film point of view?

Remender: Sure, any production work. I spent five years on feature film animation, working on *Anastasia* for three years, *Titan A.E.* briefly, then I worked on the *Iron Giant*, before moving to San Francisco to work on *Rocky and Bullwinkle* and do some commercial work for Willy Wonka candy and the Jolly Green Giant. I started my own animation studio after that, while I made underground comic books on the side. I think understanding production and understanding how things work and having done everything from writing animation, to being an animator, to storyboarding cartoons, to storyboarding video games, to writing and drawing comics, to inking comics, to printing comics—being able to understand every level of production helps me have a clear understanding of how to get my story across in a way that is realistic from a storytelling perspective and a penciling and inking perspective. Also, in terms of how production works, it has helped with reusing assets, especially in animation and video games. Being well versed in a large amount of production lingo from a variety of perspectives helps me plug myself in into almost any situation and go without having a learning curve.

Veronese: Your background makes you extremely versatile.

Remender: At the cost of my youth.

Veronese: Are there plans for any of your creator-owned projects to become video games or move into other forms of media?

Remender: Not for video games, but several in other forms. My book *Sorrow* is with the people at Twisted Evolution, the guys that made *Saw*, for a film. *Night Mary* is with Animal Magic and Summit and they are developing that for film. *Fear Agent* is being developed for film right now as well, with a director, and some big things happening with it. *Last Days of American Crime* is also moving forward, we've got a screenplay and Sam Worthington (*Avatar*, *Terminator Salvation*) is signed on to star. I think I'm missing one. There is a lot going on in regards to developing work for film, but as for video games, no. A *Fear Agent* video game would be terrific, and I've been able to scratch a little of that out in *Bulletstorm*.

Veronese: Are there any practices you see in video game storylines that frustrate you, especially as a player?

Remender: People in video games have ideas, but they are often not trained writers. That's not true in all cases; I'm casting a wide net here. Commonly, as a player, I'll be inundated with too much backstory and exposition, and people often don't know the writing rules like the classic "come late, leave early" in regards to being precise and self editing. This leads to meandering cinematics that don't immerse you, but bore you.

Veronese: I find myself tuning out of a cinematic if it lasts more than two to three minutes.

Remender: Yeah—the idea is that you are so immersed in a story that you don't want to skip a cinematic. It is all about strategically planning where they land. Not to mention anything specifically, there was one game that recently came out and was extremely well reviewed, especially for its writing as if it was a high water mark, but deep down, the writing was just meaningless relationship conflict. What I fear is that there is a generation raised on video games, a generation that doesn't know the difference between drama and melodrama and doesn't know the difference between a quality story that is engaging and manages to cut the fat versus something that is self indulgent. For example, *The Lord of the Rings* had such an extensive backstory, but it was handled in the trilogy in a two-minute sequence at the beginning of the first film, with a little exposition, excellent visuals, and only the best, most important events of the backstory told to you, and then off you went into the movie. I think the mistake a lot of people make is to write a giant story with in-depth origins and then feel the need to give you every bit of information. Instead, you need to write the backstory and have the information, but it's the 90% of the glacier under the water that moves the 10% above it. You can tell the 90% is built and is there with out it being explicitly conveyed.

Veronese: Excellent point—it seems like a lot of video game story consists of an info dump, something that is popular in prose right now, but doesn't suffice to really move things along.

Remender: The player just ends up not caring. Sometimes you need to give a big background history or touch on a character's past, but you need to do so in a concise manner that doesn't meander or languish. A lot of people spend the time writing, but they don't need to show you that stuff. They want to show you the math and the equation, but a lot of time, the equation is enough.

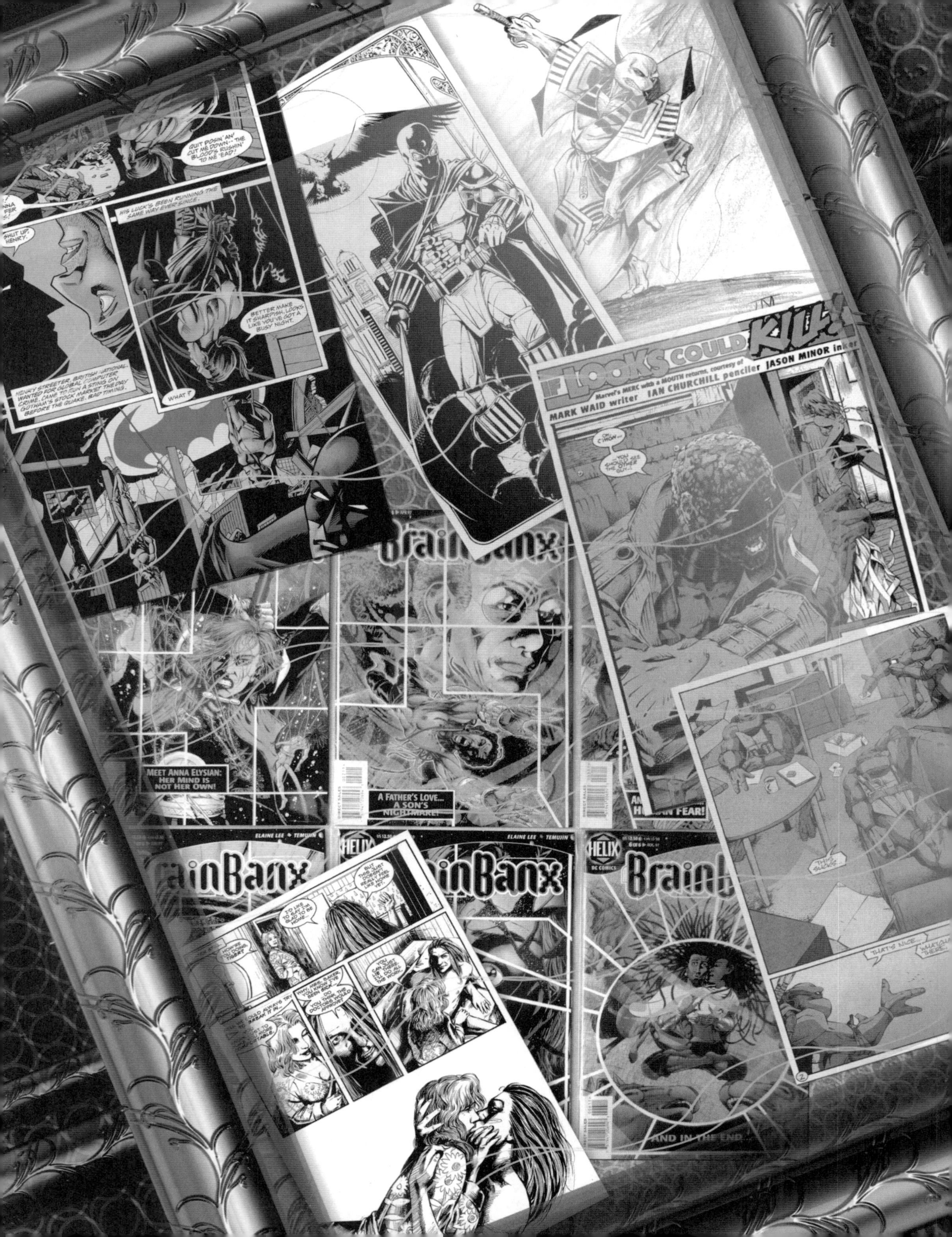
QUIT POSIN' AN' CUT ME DOWN -- THE BLOOD'S RUSHIN' TO ME 'EAD!
HIS LUCK'S BEEN RUNNING THE SAME WAY EVER SINCE.
SHUT UP, HENRY.
BETTER MAKE IT SHARPISH. LOOKS LIKE YOU'VE GOT A BUSY NIGHT.
HENRY STREETER. BRITISH NATIONAL. WANTED FOR GLOBAL COMPUTER CRIME. CAME TO RUN A STING ON GOTHAM'S STOCK MARKET THE DAY BEFORE THE QUAKE. BAD TIMING.
WHAT?
IF LOOKS COULD KILL
Marvel's MERC with a MOUTH returns, courtesy of
MARK WAID writer IAN CHURCHILL penciler JASON MINOR inker
BrainBanx
MEET ANNA ELYSIAN: HER MIND IS NOT HER OWN!
A FATHER'S LOVE... A SON'S NIGHTMARE!
ELAINE LEE • TEMUJIN
HELIX
DC COMICS
AND IN THE END...
THIS SUCKS.
THAT'S NICE...

Jason **Temujin** Minor

During his comic book career, Jason Temujin Minor penciled and inked a number of titles, including *Teenage Mutant Ninja Turtles* for Mirage Comics, the unreleased *Miracleman Triumphant* series created in the final days of Eclipse Comics, *Deadpool*, *Books of Magic*, *Buffy the Vampire Slayer*, and his creator-owned *Brain-Banx* comic for DC's Helix imprint. Minor left the world of comic books for a career in creating video games, landing a character artist position on the Sony Online Entertainment developed title *Star Wars: Galaxies* early in his video game career.

Recently, Jason Temujin Minor has worked for BioWare Austin as the lead character artist for *Star Wars: The Old Republic*, one of the most successful massively multiplayer online games in recent history. Minor is also involved in the ongoing cleanup and humanitarian efforts surrounding 2011's Fukushima Disaster , with Minor organizing comic book veterans for the charity project *Fables for Japan*.

Keith Veronese: How did you become started in working in the video game industry? What was your first project?

Jason Temujin Minor: I started working in video games in 2000.

Opposite: (l to r)
Batman: Shadow of the Bat #89, Dr. Midnight illustration, Teenage Mutant Ninja Turtles illustration, *BrainBanx #1-6*, *Deadpool: Sins of the Past #1*, *Animal Man #82* and *Teenage Mutant Ninja Turtles* Vol. 2, #2

Above:
Fables for Japan #2

I had been working as a freelance comic book artist for 10 or 11 years. However, the industry ran into some hard times. There were several factors but one of the most significant (in my opinion) was Marvel Comics' purchase of Heroes World Distribution Company. At the time, Marvel Comics distributed exclusively through Heroes World. This caused a chain reaction that shut down almost all of the other distributors and caused thousand of comic book shops to go out of business. 1999 was a very dark year for me, as jobs were sparse and I was forced to start looking for other ways to make a living. I took out a loan and bought my first computer, hoping to get into web design or video games. For the next several months, I taught myself how to use the computer and hunted for job opportunities. A friend of mine from college, Tramell Isaac, had gone into the gaming industry and was working as an Art Director at a company in Austin, Texas named Kinesoft. It took some convincing, but he eventually hired me as a concept artist. Working in the video game industry paid a hell of a lot better than working in comics. It was a whole new world for me too—I was hooked. I quickly learned 3-D modeling

CREATURE HEAD

Above:
Early concepts and model renderings

Below:
Designs for *Magelords*

and moved out of creating concept art and became a modeler. Kinesoft, unfortunately, was a doomed company and folded six months after I started working there. The game we were working on was never being released. I had seen the writing on the wall, however, and found a new job with Sony Online Entertainment about a month or two before Kinesoft closed its doors. It was unfortunate for Kinesoft, but it was a great education for me.

Veronese: It sounds like you made the best of your opportunities for on the job training. How did you become involved with *Star Wars Galaxies* at Sony Online Entertainment? What games did you work on during that time?

Minor: It started when I was working in Austin at Kinesoft, on a game called *Magelords*. Things weren't looking that good with the project so I started looking elsewhere. I heard about another video game in production in the Austin by another developer. It was a *Star Wars* project that was expected to be the next *Everquest*. It sounded like one hell of a job, so I put in my resume. I didn't hear anything for a while so I kept looking. Another

company had just made me an offer when Sony On-line Entertainment got in touch. They wanted to interview me for a position in San Diego. It turns out that the *Star Wars* development was split between San Diego and Austin. I kept the other company waiting while I met with Sony Online Entertainment. The interview went well and they eventually made me an offer. The other company was remarkably understanding when I told them I was going to work at Sony Online Entertainment in San Diego, but I think they were a little pissed. Four years later, after *Star Wars Galaxies* had shipped, Sony Online Entertainment shut down the San Diego *Star Wars* team and moved me back to Austin, where I had originally applied and worked previously.

Veronese: How did you become associated with BioWare? What has your role been on *Star Wars: Old Republic*?

Minor: The BioWare Austin team, the team that is making *Star Wars: The Old Republic*, was founded by several of us who worked on *Star Wars Galaxies*. Most of the original artists came from *Star Wars Galaxies* and BioWare relocated their chief Design and Writing teams from Canada to Austin for this project. I was hired from Sony when the project started up and was eventually made the Lead Character Artist. My team's responsibilities are to create the player characters, the non-player characters (story and quest characters), droids, and creatures for the game. We build the assets and then work with the animators to get them skinned up, animated, and ready for the game.

Veronese: What was it like being present at the ground floor of BioWare Austin?

Minor: I joined BioWare Austin about a year after they started up, but I'd been talking with them from the start. It was interesting. We were a small

team, about thirty people, and we had not officially signed the contracts for *Star Wars: The Old Republic* (in fact it wasn't even called that at the time). We were working on the game anyway and hoped the contracts did not fall through. It was fun. We were still trying to figure out what we wanted the game to look like and how we wanted to tackle it. We were also trying to wrap our heads around the size of the project. I don't think any of us understood how big BioWare Austin would get. The team is now around four hundred and growing and we've moved offices twice now to accommodate the size of the team.

Veronese: Was staying within the *Star Wars* universe a plus in working at BioWare?

Minor: *Star Wars* was not so much of a draw for me. I am a fan but one of the last projects I worked on in comics was a *Star Wars* book, and then I spent six years on *Galaxies*. That tends to numb you a little to the *Star Wars* mystique. The draw to Austin was that I really liked the art team being put together and BioWare gave us a chance to make the game we set out to create when we were making *Star Wars Galaxies*.

Veronese: What is a typical day for you like at BioWare? Do you work in an office or from home?

Minor: I work in an office. Most of the video game industry works standard, daytime hours in an office. However, there is more of a push these days to use freelancers. Often, this means outsourcing work to studios, but sometimes they work with free-lancers who work from home.

My days are a little unpredictable. I am a lead artist, so I'm usually in meetings, tracking down issues, providing feedback, and doing what I can to make

Above:
Star Wars Galaxies game art

sure my team can do their jobs. I have a team of six artists that work in-house and 10 to 20 outsourced artists that are working on the characters. That's a lot of people to keep track of at the end of the day.

The first thing I do when I get to the office is to look over the messaging forums we use to communicate with our outsourcing studios. I look to see what assets they have dropped and then I assign these "drops" to my in-house team so they can provide the outsourcers with feedback. I'll do some of the feedback myself if I have the time or if the in-house team is swamped.

After that, I look at what needs to be done that day, which can vary a good deal. Maybe it is bug fixing, maybe it is conferring with the concept department or writing department to determine what assets additional are needed, or maybe it is spending the day in a Microsoft Excel spreadsheet working out the schedule for our next milestone. I check to make sure my team's needs are taken care of and provide guidance on the work they are doing. There is usually a meeting or two each day I attend as well. After that, if there is any time left in the day, I might get to do a little art myself. So far, I've done very little art on *Star Wars: The Old Republic* project. My responsibilities are mostly management and scheduling.

Veronese: Using private forums for asset dropping is rather advanced. Are the outsourced assets usually environmental or detail art?

Minor: We have one outsource studio in China that handles the environment art assets and another in Russia that we use for character assets. The Russian studio is the one I manage.

Veronese: Was there a learning curve in moving to more of a managerial role at BioWare or was it something that you grew into over time?

Minor: I had been the character lead and then the art director on *Star Wars Galaxies*, so I had already had my introduction to acting is a management role by the time I started BioWare. However, there is always a learning curve when you join a new company. Everybody has their own way of doing things.

Veronese: You mentioned debugging—what is the debugging process like? Is it a series of notations or actual programming?

Minor: The process is a little different depending on which team you are on. Art, design, and programming all have their own process. We have a whole quality assurance team of testers that constantly run through the game and document any bugs they find. The bugs are collected and sorted in a program called DevTrack. Any art bugs relating to the creatures or characters are funneled down to me and then I hand them out to my team to fix. Often we schedule a day a week to fix bugs so we can keep on top of them without bogging us down and blocking the other tasks we have.

Veronese: Have you been involved with any other projects while at BioWare Austin?

Minor: No, this project is the largest game BioWare has ever made. I've been working on it since I was hired four years ago.

Veronese: Are you working on any comic book-related projects? Would you like to return to comics one day?

Minor: I enjoy my work in the video game industry, but comics will always be my first love. Unfortunately, the money that video game work pays has spoiled me, and I now have a wife and a baby on the way. Financially, I would have to make some pretty big adjustments to go back to working freelance in the comics industry. Also, the older I get, the harder it is for me to keep the kind of work schedule comics required. Making games has it own trials and tribulations, but the hours are nowhere near as bad as when I was working in comics.

However, I do have a few small comic projects ongoing that I'm working on in my spare time, but nothing that is ready for print yet. I'm also writing and trying to get that published, and working on some children's books with my wife.

Veronese: What kind of fiction writing do you do? That, combined with the experience of creating children's books has to be a nice change of pace from video game work.

Minor: So far I haven't written to one genre exclusively. I am currently working on a modern pulp detective story that runs every month in a local publication called the *Gabriel Writer*. Also, a short story of mine recently won the grand prize in a statewide writing contest. Prose makes for a very nice change. I enjoy making games, but comics and storytelling has always been what I've enjoyed the most.

Veronese: Do you play video games?

Minor: This is the question that always results in disappointment for gamers when I answer, no, I do not play video games. It's not an entirely true answer; I do play games as research for my job and to keep up on what's happening in the industry. I can't remember the last game I played a game to completion. I did play *City of Heroes* for a while, but the last game I played purely for fun was probably *Abe's Odyssey*. It's a bit dated now, but I thought it was very well done.

Veronese: You were trained at the Kubert School. Was there one particular piece of knowledge

bestowed there that has really stuck with you and you continue to apply?

Minor: There were many. The Kubert School was a fantastic place to learn. I guess the one piece of knowledge that sticks out the most was something one of my teachers, Kim DeMulder, said on my first day. You have to understand, the Kubert School is filled with comic book collectors and freaks, and I was no exception. Kim started his class by taking out a comic book and shaking it. He then proceeded to fold back the cover, crease it, and break the spine. There were audible gasps in the room—some of them angry. The collectors were horribly offended that Kim would treat a comic this way. He looked at us and said, "I read my comics like this because I am not a collector and neither are you, not any more. You are no longer consumers. From this point on, you are creators." His point was that we had to change our mind set. We had to let go of our inner fanboy and learn the basics of drafting. Only then can you understand why an artist does what they do instead of blindly mimicking them. This has been the biggest help to me in my professional career. Most of the time when I see a young artist's work that just is not hitting the professional level it is because they are trying to mimic their favorite artist instead of taking the time to learn why that artist is successful. At some point, you have to let the fanboy part of yourself go and become your own artist. This applies to anything creative, not just comics. I see similar situations in video games all the time.

Opposite & Above:
Star Wars: The Old Republic promotional art

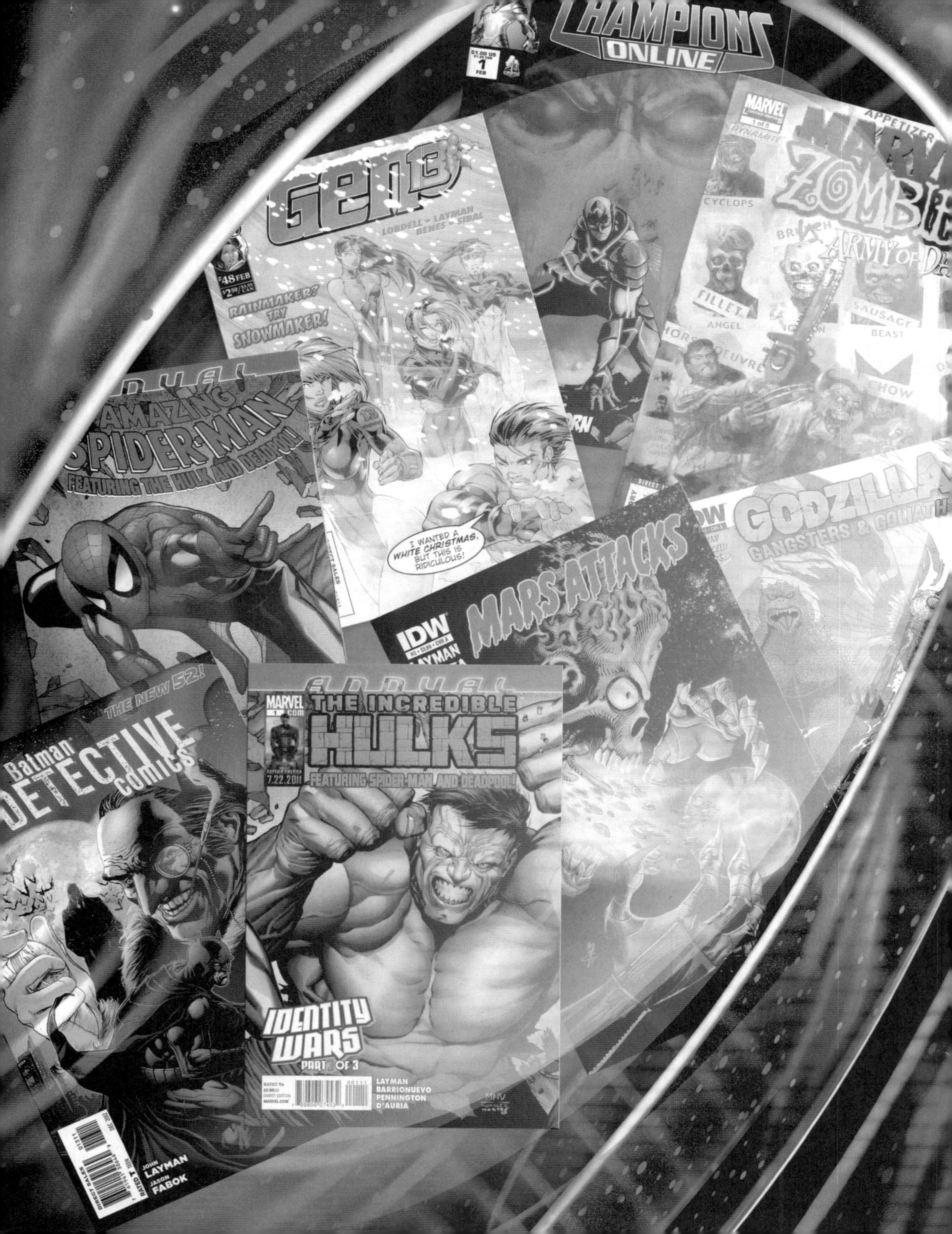

CHAMPIONS ONLINE
$1.00 US
1
FEB
Gen13
LOBDELL • LAYMAN
BENES • SIBAL
#48 FEB
$2.50
RAINMAKER? TRY SNOWMAKER!
I WANTED A WHITE CHRISTMAS, BUT THIS IS RIDICULOUS!
MARVEL
1 of 5
DYNAMITE
APPETIZER
MARVEL ZOMBIES vs. ARMY OF DARKNESS
CYCLOPS
FILLET
ANGEL
SAUSAGE
BEAST
CHOW
ANNUAL
AMAZING SPIDER-MAN
FEATURING THE HULK AND DEADPOOL!
IDW
GODZILLA
GANGSTERS & GOLIATHS
MARS ATTACKS
IDW
LAYMAN
THE NEW 52!
Batman
DETECTIVE COMICS
JOHN LAYMAN
JASON FABOK
DIRECT SALES
ANNUAL
MARVEL
THE INCREDIBLE HULKS
FEATURING SPIDER-MAN AND DEADPOOL!
7.22.2011
IDENTITY WARS
PART 1 OF 3
LAYMAN
BARRIONUEVO
PENNINGTON
D'AURIA
MARVEL.COM

John**Layman**

John Layman began his comic book career as an editor at Wildstorm Comics and quickly took up writing reins on *Gen 13* before moving on to write for Marvel and DC. During the mid-2000s, John began writing video games for Cryptic Studios, which we will talk about candidly in this interview.

Layman is currently helming the widely successful *Chew*, a creator-owned comic published by Image and drawn by the amazing Rob Guillory. *Chew* tells the story of Tony Chu, a former Philadelphia cop who now works for the Food and Drug Administration. While this appears to be a mundane job at first glance, Chu works as a special agent for the FDA, gaining psychic impressions that help him solve cases by eating food and even people. Eating people is not foreign territory to Layman, as he wrote the intercompany crossover *Marvel Zombies vs. The Army of Darkness*. Showtime is currently developing a half-hour television series based on *Chew*.

Keith Veronese: You started working in the comic industry in the late '90s in an editorial capacity, but began scripting in 2000-01 (*Gen 13*) and expanded with the *Gambit* ongoing series in 2004. What drew you to a career in comics? Was writing always a goal, or something that initially grew out of an editorial necessity to meet deadlines?

John Layman: I had always wanted to write comics. From my earliest memories in childhood, it has been my *only* goal. Being an English major in school, going into journalism, becoming a comic book editor—this was all work I did to try to get closer to writing comics. There was no Internet back then, and I hadn't the slightest idea how things were supposed to be done.

Opposite:
Champions Online #1,
Marvel Zombies #1, Godzilla:
Gangsters and Goliaths #2,
Mars Attacks #2, The
Incredible Hulks Annual #1,
Detective Comics #13,
The Amazing Spider-Man
Annual #38 and Gen 13 #48
Above:
Chew #13

Veronese: What has been your most enjoyable experience during your career so far in comics?

Layman: It probably has to be *Chew*, which is not just creatively gratifying, but also commercially. Not only that, I own the damn thing.

Veronese: You were involved with Cryptic Studios, originators of *City of Heroes*, along with *Champions Online* and *Star Trek Online*. How did you become involved with and what was your role at Cryptic?

CITY OF HEROES
TEEN
NCSOFT
CRYPTIC STUDIOS

Layman: At a time when my wife's newspaper job was in question, and I had just done a couple of very frustrating comic book jobs, I seemed to stumble from one video game job to the next without really trying. This culminated in an offer from Cryptic Studios, based on a recommendation that came from Microsoft and Brian Michael Bendis. The offer from Cryptic was a position as their in-house writer, with most of my work geared toward a collaboration with Bendis on what would have become the Marvel MMO. After all, at that point in my career I had written comics, written video games, and written for Marvel. Plus, I was willing to relocate to California, so I seemed perfect for the gig.

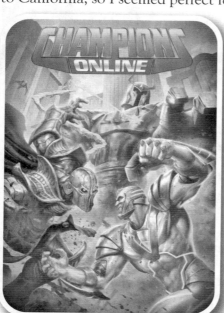

Veronese: Was *Champions Online* initially going to be the Marvel/Microsoft venture, *Marvel Universe Online*?

CHAMPIONS
ONLINE

Layman: Yep, that is why I relocated for the job; just a few months after Microsoft pulled the plug. I tried to turn lemons into lemonade by sticking around and doing *Champions Online*.

PlayStation.2
Cabela's
DANGEROUS
HUNTS
TEEN
ACTIVISION

Veronese: A lot of video game work goes without being properly credited or publicized, especially writing work. Have there been any other games have you worked on?

Layman: Yeah, I got my start with Activision and their subsidiary Activision Value Publishing. A friend of mine who worked at Nintendo was recommended for a game, and could not do it because it was a conflict of interest. I got recommended for the job—a *Cabela's Dangerous Hunts* extreme hunting game. That led to scripting work for a handful of other licensed Activision games including *World Series of Poker*, *American Chopper*, and *History Channel's Civil War*. At some point word got back to Nintendo that Activision was happy with me, and that was good. That led to me working on a *Metroid DS* game and a Wii game that was scuttled before it ever saw the light of day. Also, somewhere between Activision, Nintendo, and Cryptic I worked on the *Marvel Trading Card Game* for the PSP that Konami put out based the physical game Marvel created.

Veronese: Are you doing any video game work currently?

Layman: Nope, strangely, while *Chew* has gone on to surprising success, the video game work has dried up.

Veronese: More time to dedicate to *Chew* then, that's not a bad thing. Congrats for winning an Eisner Award for *Chew* by the way! How long was the concept for *Chew* brewing before it developed into a series?

Layman: Years and years and years. I'd say close to a half decade.

Veronese: What are some of the challenges in writing for games (especially large scale role-playing games like MMORPGs) compared to an individual

Above Left: *City of Heroes* packaging

Above Right: *Cabela's Dangerous Hunts* packaging

Left: *Champions Online* packaging

comic title?

Layman: That is hard to put a definite finger on. There are a lot of chefs in the kitchen with video games. You often find yourself in a situation where you write a lot of stuff that gets changed or altered or thrown out altogether for game play reasons. But that is just the nature of the beast. In my experience, I was collaborating with fewer people than you would in comics, and therefore, I think there is more of a sense of ownership. The money, day-to-day, is much better in video games, though, but I've also found the bar for quality is much lower. That is, I had to clean up a lot of truly lousy writing in video games, where to even break in the door in mainstream comics the quality bar is far, far higher.

Veronese: What did your journalistic career center on? How long were you a journalist?

Layman: Well, I was straight out of college, so I was more of a "Jimmy Olsen"-type news assistant, de-livering mail and eventually working up to being the guy who designed the charts and graphs for the business section. I also had an opportunity to freelance too, and I got to do a lot of pop culture stuff, music, science-fiction news, and comics-related articles.

Veronese: How did your first writing job in comics come about?

Layman: Scott Lobdell went missing in action when a *GEN 13* script was due, so I jumped in and finished it up.

Veronese: What did your scripting work, especially for non-genre, licensed games like *Cabela's Dangerous Hunts* entail? What was the writing process like? How long did scripting for a typical game take?

Layman: Each game was different. Some took months with a lot of back and forth between myself the developer. Some games I was able to polish over a weekend or a week. And I can't really speak to process specifics, because it really changed from game to game. It's a good thing I am able to roll with the punches…

Veronese: How was your experience writing for *Champions Online*? What kind of writing did you do?

Layman: Every-thing. Anything and everything. My writing work for *Champions Online* ranged from coming up with punny mission names and power and item names, to overarching fiction for the entire game, to dialogue for all mission contacts, including non-player

characters and triggered spawns. There was nothing that was really off limits when it came to what I was given the opportunity to write for with *Champions Online*. I wrote whatever was needed, whatever they asked me too, and there was enough variety that the job never really got dull.

Veronese: What was a typical day on staff at Cryptic Studios like?

Layman: Well, you show up in an office, and your workday is split between meeting and writing. I was sort of at the "beck and call" of a lot of designers. They would tell me what they needed, and I would either provide a script for them, or a ideas for whatever zone or instance they were working on at the moment.

Above Left:
Metroid Prime Hunters packaging

Above Right:
American Chopper packaging

Left:
Marvel Trading Card Game art

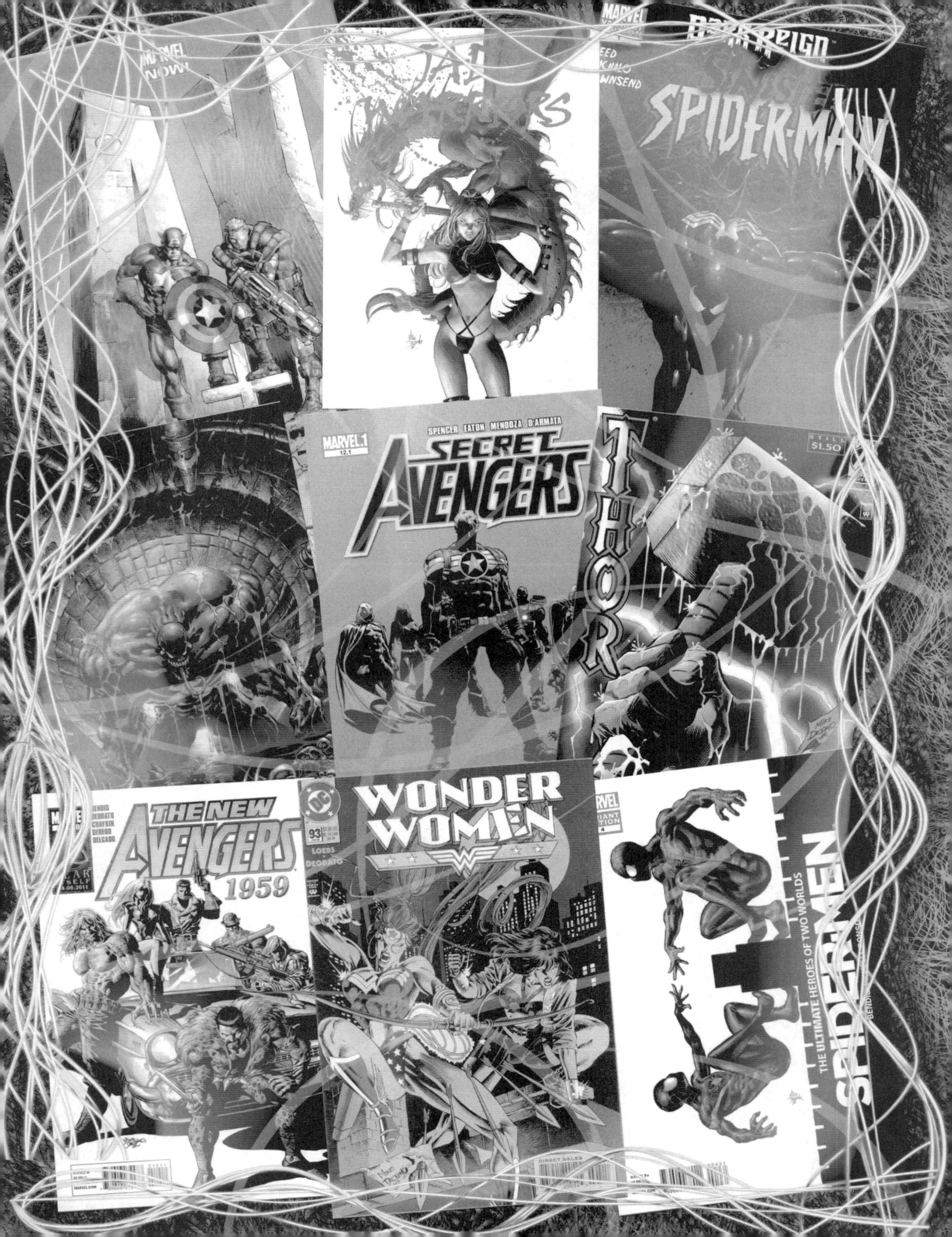
MARVEL NOW!
SPIDER-MAN
SPENCER EATON MENDOZA D'ARMATA
MARVEL.1
12.1
SECRET AVENGERS
THOR
STILL $1.50
BENDIS
DEODATO
CHAYKIN
BEREDO
DELGADO
THE NEW AVENGERS
1959
WONDER
93
LOEDS
DEODATO
MARVEL
THE ULTIMATE HEROES OF TWO WORLDS
SPIDER-MEN
DIRECT SALES
MARVEL.COM

Mike**Deodato**

Mike Deodato's two-decade plus comic book career reads like a who's who of the superhero universe— a magnificent *Wonder Woman* run early in his career, an extended stint on several *Avengers* titles including *New Avengers* and *Dark Avengers*, along with time on *Amazing Spider-Man* and the *Incredible Hulk*.

Mike recently teamed up with Zen Studios and Sony Computer Entertainment to create cut scenes for *Punisher: No Mercy*, a first-person shooter released via the PlayStation Network.

Keith Veronese: How were you approached to work on *The Punisher: No Mercy?*

Mike Deodato: With great caution and trepidation, because with my lightning-fast lethal martial arts hands, I can be deadly! (Laughs) Former Marvel talent coordinator Chris Allo approached me about the gaming job and, despite my crazy busy schedule, I said *yes*! Then when I discovered how much work it was—well, you haven't heard from Chris Allo since, have you? (Laughs) Seriously, Chris was a great guy. Saw him last in Toronto at a con, a year or so ago.

Veronese: What was the extent of your work on *Punisher: No Mercy?*

Deodato: In its development stages, the game was called *Punisher: War Zone*. Justin Lambros of Marvel Studios approached me to illustrate for the game, for their Marvel Interactive division. It was inspired, of course, by the movie of that name, although the characters were to look like the comic books rather than film versions of the characters. So they bore a lot of similarities to Marvel's MAX line.

In that sense, I was hired to draw roughly 50 panels of art. The art is basically a series of comic strips to be incorporated into the game through cut scenes and transmissions.

Veronese: *The Punisher: No Mercy* was developed solely for distribution via

Opposite: (left to right)
A vs. X #1, Jade Warriors, Dark Reign: Sinister Spider-Man #1, Venom #12, Secret Avengers #12.1, Thor #494, The New Avengers #10, Wonder Woman #93 and Spider-Men #4

Above:
Punisher: Force of Nature #1

download, and downloadable content is usually produced on a shorter time table than retail video games. How long did you work on *Punisher: No Mercy?*

Deodato: About three months, but not steadily. I was drawing this between issues the artwork for *The Punisher: No Mercy* in between receiving Warren Ellis scripts for *Thunderbolts.*

The game designers told me they were going for the same tone as the movie in lighting, in music, and so forth. They had already built arenas set in a glass recycling plant and at the docks that were inspired by the movie as well. Also, in addition to the normal characters like The Punisher, Jigsaw, and Microchip, the game also includes Barracuda, Finn Cooley, Jenny Cesare, Bushwacker, and Silver Sable.

The Punisher: War Zone is an arena-style first-person shooter. When I was brought on the project I was told, "Think *Goldeneye* for the Nintendo 64 as a good point of reference." As I understand it, it was to be available for download over the PlayStation 3's PlayStation Network, Windows Live on PCs, and maybe Xbox Live Arcade on Xbox 360. At least that was their plan; I don't know if that changed in the process. This was a new kind of game for the Marvel Interactive division, as they were working directly with the development team, so it was important for them to have, as they said, the "Authentic Marvel Comics stamp on the artwork."

Veronese: What was the main difference between working on a video game versus a comic book?

Deodato: I didn't have to consider placement of word balloon and captions. It was just artwork. Being a commercial job rather than a monthly comic, it had the usual additional approval level. In other words, the art went through a lot of checkpoints and was seen by a number of people before being approved. On the upside, my regular colorist, Rainier Beredo, got to work on the gaming art, as well.

Veronese: Have you worked much on the Punisher in the past?

Deodato: Weren't you paying attention? For *The Punisher,* I've already drawn several covers as well as issue four of volume two of *Punisher War Journal,* written by Matt Fraction. Remember these martial arts hands, man...

Veronese: Your cover to *Punisher: Forces of Nature* is easily one of the best covers of the decade. It's epic... literally. Things don't get much more epic than the Punisher fighting a sperm whale. What kind of direction were you given in drawing the cover?

Deodato: As I recall, Marvel suggested that I give the cover "a feel like Moby Dick"—a story of some nut chasing a big fish, I guess. So I went all-out put the crazy guy in a little boat with only a spear facing off with the massive whale. I made it clear this wasn't Pinocchio going down Monstro's gullet for a heart-to-heart with Gepetto! (Laughs)

Veronese: Why do you think video game developers are reaching out to comic artists? A Punisher game is a natural extension/transition from comic books, but video game publishers (particularly Electronic Arts) seem to be pursuing comic artists and writers on a regular basis

to develop new intellectual properties.

Deodato: Well, it only makes sense. Who would know comics characters better than comics creators? Plus, in some cases, there's the "name value" of the comic book talent that may prove to be an additional incentive for certain collectors.

Veronese: Do you play video games? Did you get to play an early version of *The Punisher: No Mercy* while working on it?

Deodato: No, not really. The last game I played was on the Atari. Of course, my friend Dave has challenged me to some bowling on the Wii when I visit him this Christmas. Will that count?

Veronese: Are you working on any other video game projects in the future?

Deodato: That depends. They've got my number, and I'm happy to do more games if the schedules allow and the planets are in the right alignment.

Now if you'll excuse me, I gotta go shatter some boards and bricks with my bare hands....

Veronese: What sort of direction were you given in drawing the panels art for *Punisher: No Mercy*? Were you working off of a script or a general plot? If so, who wrote the script?

Deodato: I was, as usual, given a full script when I worked on the art for *Punisher: No Mercy*. All of the art was broken down page by page, panel by panel, with the descriptions and dialogue included as well. The game was written by Chris Baker, with whom I've not worked before.

Veronese: The panels you drew for *Punisher: No Mercy* helped comprise the storyline of the single player portion of the game. What was your favorite part of the storyline to draw?

Deodato: The opening sequence, down at the docks. Not only were there explosions and interesting visuals to draw, it was loaded with Frank Castle,

Barracuda, and Silver Sable, so the characters were interesting. The characters were also always in motion, so that made it more fun to draw.

Veronese: What was it like working on a movie tie-in? Had you seen *Punisher: War Zone* prior to working on *Punisher: No Mercy*?

Deodato: Working on the game wasn't a different experience for me at all. It is not as though they gave me any actor references or even sent me a DVD of the movie. Come to think of it, I still haven't seen the movie!

Veronese: Have you been approached to do video game work in the past?

Deodato: I could swear I did some storyboards many years ago for another video game, but for the life of me I don't remember the specifics.

Veronese: Do you have a dream video game project?

Deodato: Absolutely, and it would be *Jade Warriors*. *Jade Warriors* is a miniseries I co-created years ago at Image Comics, about a team of sexy female assassins controlled by the Yakuza. It involved mythical dragons rising up to destroy Japan, it had action galore, it had characters of mine like Ramthar that I'd created in the '80s and published in Brazil, it had a character called Deathkiss. It was a lot of fun and it was also the first and only time in American comics I've been involved in plotting a book I drew.

While we're at it, I'd love to see someone collect and publish my whole *Jade Warriors* project as a graphic novel. We're coming up on its 15th Anniversary, and there are two unpublished issues!

Above:
The Punisher: No Mercy concept art

Above:
The Punisher: No Mercy screenshots

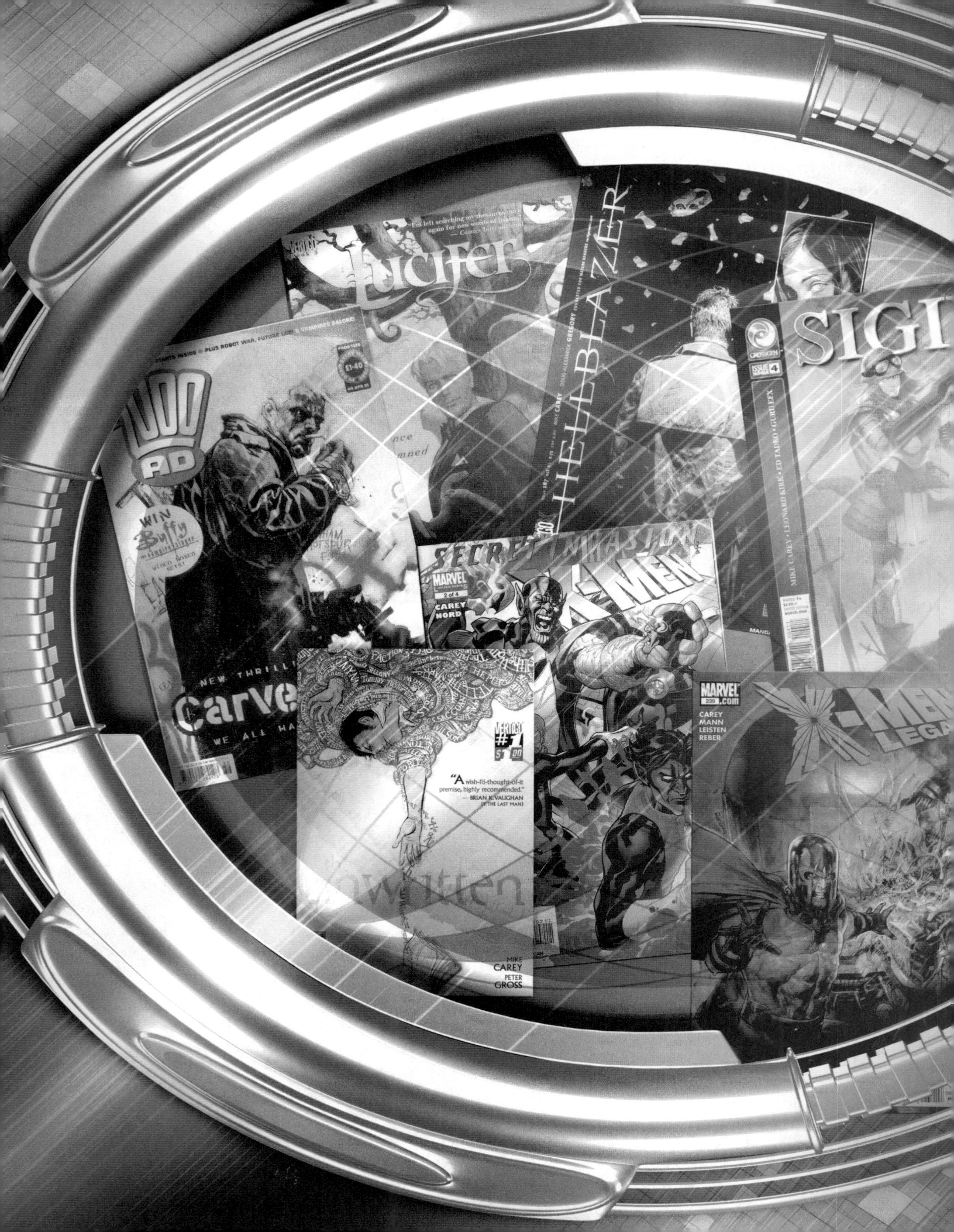

Lucifer
HELLBLAZER
MIKE CAREY
ISSUE 4
MIKE CAREY • LEONARD KIRK • ED TADEO • GURU EFX
WIN Buffy the Vampire Slayer VIDEO BOXED SETS!
£1·40
SECRET INVASION
X-MEN
MARVEL
2 of 4
CAREY
NORD
VERTIGO
"A wish-I'd-thought-of-it premise, highly recommended."
— BRIAN K. VAUGHAN
[Y: THE LAST MAN]
MIKE
CAREY
PETER
GROSS
MARVEL
239
.com
CAREY
MANN
LEISTEN
REBER

Mike**Carey**

Mike Carey started off as many English comic book writers do, working for the British comic book institution that is *2000 AD*. His first mainstream North American work came under DC's Vertigo imprint where he wrote *Lucifer* and did a forty-issue writing stint on *Hellblazer*. Carey helped architect Marvel's 2008 *Secret Invasion* crossover and regularly writes *X-Men: Legacy* as well as the creator-owned *The Unwritten*.

In addition to work in the comic book industry, Carey has written several novels revolving around Felix Castor, a freelance exorcist and ghost hunter, including *The Devil You Know*. Mike Carey worked on a very incarnation of the first installment of the *Fable* series, one of the first video games that allowed players to take a moral stance and significantly change the playing experience.

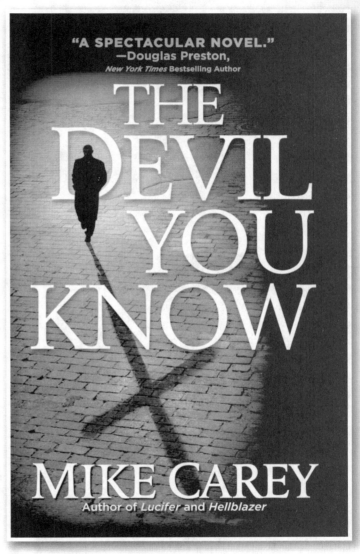

"A SPECTACULAR NOVEL."
—Douglas Preston,
New York Times Bestselling Author

THE DEVIL YOU KNOW

MIKE CAREY

Author of *Lucifer* and *Hellblazer*

Keith Veronese: What can you tell us about the video game projects you have worked on?

Mike Carey: Not a whole hell of a lot! It's standard to be made to sign a non-disclosure agreement on this kind of work.

Veronese: If you need to be vague, that is no problem. What type of video game projects did you work on? Were they comic adaptations or new intellectual properties?

Carey: A mixture of both, but usually with the video game company as the leading partner, so to speak. I've never approached a game company with a

Opposite: (clockwise)
2000 AD: Carvel Hale,
Lucifer #3 TPB,
Hellblazer #187, Sigil #4,
X-Men #239,
X-Men: Secret Invasion
#2 and The Unwritten #1

Above:
The Devil You Know

concept of my own. It's always been a case of being approached to work on a specific project that's already in the works.

Veronese: Did you do plot and story work or strictly dialogue work?

Carey: I did both. The first time I worked on a video game, it was for the developer Big Blue Box (a satellite of Lionhead Studios), for the game that eventually became *Fable*. I only did very "broad strokes" plot work there, with this all taking place at a very early stage of the process. Big Blue Box already knew how the game was going to work, but were looking to solidify an over-arching storyline. I provided some ideas, but I don't know if any of them were eventually used.

More recently, I did story work and cutscene scripting for an Electronic Arts game. I am now heavily involved (along with another writer) in the writing of the main script and in-game script for another major game company. So I guess over time I have become more involved in the nuts-and-bolts writing, which is both the most fun and the most challenging part of the job.

Veronese: How is writing for video games different than writing for comics? How does it compare to

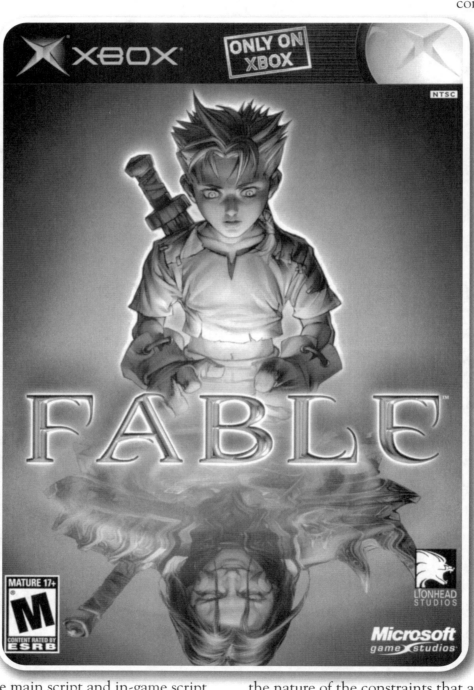

the novels you have written?

Carey: Writing for video games is more comparable to writing a screenplay, in that every creative decision is also a budgetary decision. If you bring in a new character, a new setting, a new scene, there are cost implications and technical considerations. With a comic book or a novel you have an infinite budget, pretty much by definition and the nature of the medium.

It's also different in that with a game, you are kind of writing from inside Schrödinger's box: different states of the narrative can co-exist, and you're writing scenarios that are mutually incompatible because they can still happen depending on the decisions that the player makes. The wave form hasn't collapsed.

Veronese: Was there more or less freedom while working on a video game?

Carey: It is probably not a case of more versus less—it's the nature of the constraints that are there, and how you encounter them. If you write on a comic book franchise, there are still limits on what you can do with the characters and how you can pull the story in a specific direction. It's all done by negotiation, and the same is true for a console game. With a game, though, there is more of a sense of the financial structures, the fact that you're working within a budget. I can be blithely ignorant of money when I'm writing a comic or a novel—and I generally am.

Veronese: How were you initially approached to do video game work? Was there any initial interest in the field?

Carey: In each case the approach came through either my UK agent or my blog site.

Veronese: Creatively, how did you feel about non-disclosure agreements? Are they typical for all video game story work or are they contingent on the game being published?

Carey: I imagine they're typical for all work on big media franchises. If I remember rightly, I had to sign non-disclosure agreements when I wrote the comic book adaptation of the first *Fantastic Four* movie, because, when I starting writing the adaptation, it was before the movie was actually released. It seems only reasonable to me that producers take steps to keep their stories under wraps until they're ready to release information. I've never objected to signing a non-disclosure agreement.

Veronese: During what time period did you work on the game that eventually became *Fable*?

Carey: I don't even remember. But it was very early on and the game didn't then have a name. [**Author's note**: *This probably puts the time of Mike's work around or prior to 2002, when* Fable *was being*

created under the name Project Ego.]

Veronese: How long are you involved on a particular game?

Carey: It varies from a few months to about a year.

Veronese: Do you play video games?

Carey: I do, but I play *old* video games—1980s platformers like *Sonic the Hedgehog*. I don't have the time to play the big, modern, total-immersion games. I barely have the time to read a newspaper these days.

Veronese: Are there any comics projects you have worked on in the past that you think would make for a good video game?

Carey: I think any self-contained story with a strong pay-off ought to translate easily to video games. *Voodoo Child* (a book written by Carey based on characters created by Nicholas Cage and his son Weston), possibly. Or *Spellbinders* (a six-issue mini-series Carey did with Mike Perkins for Marvel Comics that takes place in Salem, Massachusetts, a locale often associated with magic), with its magical lineages and visually defined spells.

Opposite:
Fable package art

Above:
Fable screenshot

Left:
Voodoo Child #1

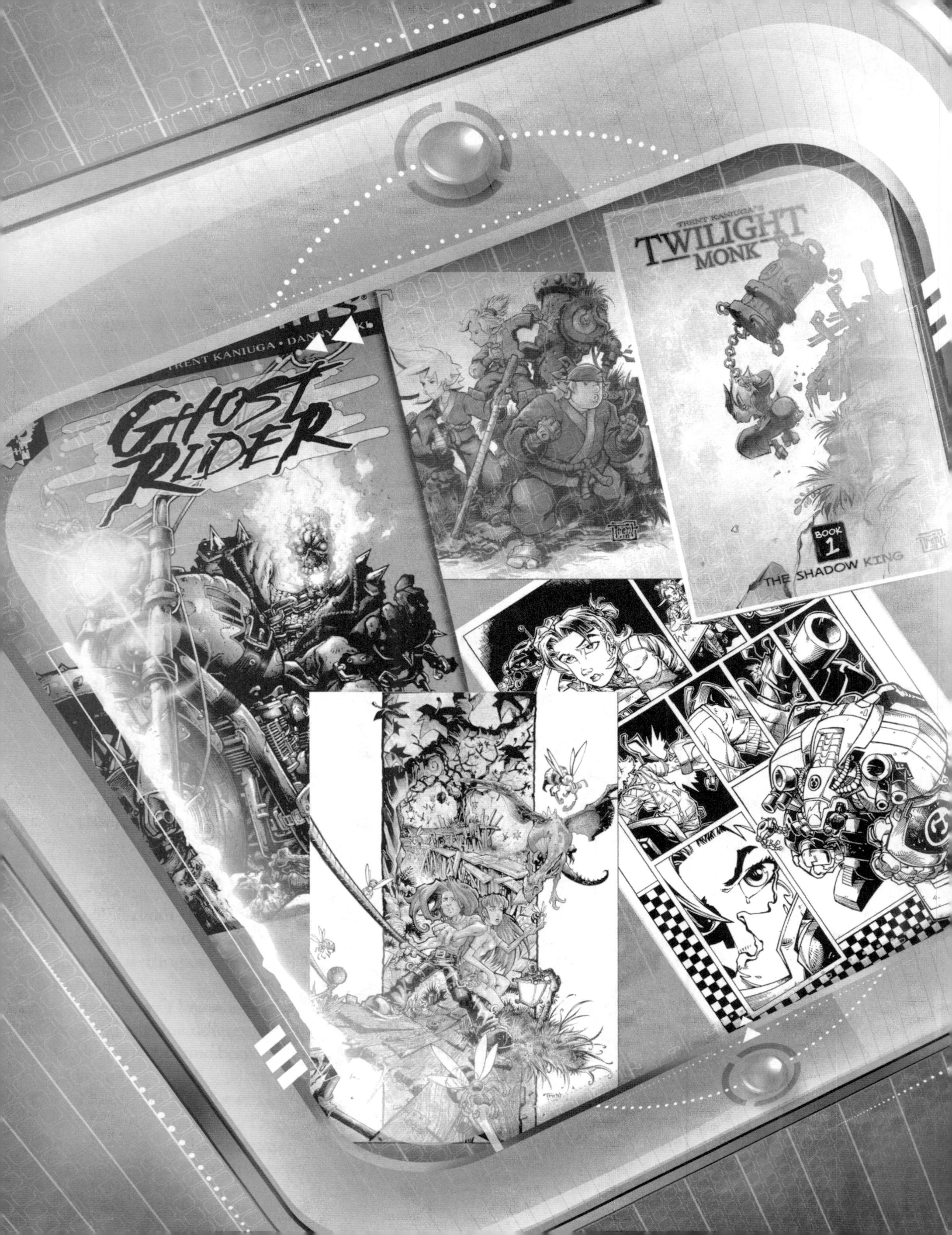
TRENT KANIUGA
GHOST RIDER
TRENT KANIUGA'S
TWILIGHT
MONK
BOOK 1
THE SHADOW KING

Trent**Kaniuga**

Kaniuga is the teenage wunderkind behind *CreeD*, a hit independent series in the 1990s. Trent later moved to Marvel Comics, where he worked on a revival of *Ghost Rider* for the Marvel Knights line. Kaniuga left the day-to-day comic book world and entered the world of video game creation in 2002, working as an art director for several Game Boy Advance titles before taking a position at the foremost company in PC gaming, Blizzard, where created concept and environment art for *World of WarCraft* and one of the most anticipated games of the decade, *Diablo III*.

Trent still loves making comics, releasing the creator-owned *Nova Colony* and *Twilight Monk* as well as a 500+ page tome collecting all of his *CreeD* stories, *CreeD: Omnichronos*.

CREED
OMNICHRONOS
THE COMPLETE COLLECTION

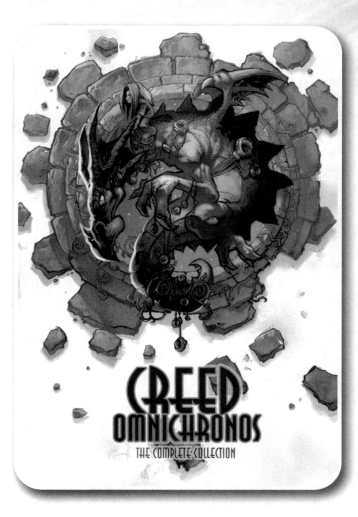

Keith Veronese: You have had a very successful comic book career, from the creator-owned hit *CreeD* to *Ghost Rider* to covers for the Marvel Knights line. What are some of the reasons that led you to working in video games full-time?

Trent Kaniuga: Babies… mostly. That and LCD televisions, nice clothes, and a desire to live in a neighborhood where I would not get stabbed. I grew up very poor, and I was presented with an opportunity to build a career in an industry that I had always dreamed of working in, and in the process make a steady paycheck. I think I always thought that I would eventually become a creator in the video game industry, but I keep getting sidetracked with great opportunities to work on already really successful franchises. Thank you for your compliment, but I don't really know if I would call my career in comics all that "successful." I had always hoped to do a thirty-to-forty-

Opposite: (l to r) *Marvel Knights: Ghost Rider* #1, *CreeD* illustration, *Twilight Monk* #1, *CreeD* #1, *Bombshell* page

Above: *CreeD: Omnichronos*

issue run on a series, but I never really got to do so. I still hope to someday. I think I just want to do everything, which is why I do both comics and games. Comics can be very… sporadic in an economic manner. With free-lance work in general, you are always looking for the next gig, and sometimes you go for four months between paychecks, and sometimes you have to do projects just to make sure the bills are paid. Working in the video game industry fulfills my creative interests, while at the same time affording me a comfortable lifestyle.

Veronese: Was this your first video game work?

Kaniuga: My first video game work was painting 16-bit rocks for a Game Boy Advance *He-Man: Power of Greyskull* game at a small startup studio. That led to doing all of the background tiles for a *Terminator 3: Rise of the Machines* Game Boy Advance game, and then I was able to act as an art director, creating pitches and demos for our studio's next project. One of the producers at Capcom was very interested in stealing me away from working on Game Boy Advance games and have me do concept art and direct some cut scenes, and that also gave me to opportunity to redesign the *Maximo* characters and world that Capcom owned.

Veronese: You were a voice actor for 2006's *Final Fight: Streetwise* and handled the writing and art chores for the accompanying comic.

Above:
Final Fight: Streetwise

Right:
Final Fight: Streetwise concept art

Opposite:
World of WarCraft: Wrath of the Lich King

How did your involvement with the project come about?

Kaniuga: *Maximo* was cancelled as a series, and Capcom Japan directed us to make an "American Style" urban-gangster game based on the *Final Fight* series. Early on, I was doing temporary voice work for the main character, Kyle Travers, and… I guess I was about 26, the same age as the character. I smoked a lot, and drank a lot, so my voice was just about perfect for the kind of character that we were making. And just like the character, I was also quite popular with the ladies I might add… (ahem). Anyway, the team really pushed for me to do the voice, even though I wasn't a union voice actor. I was very nervous about doing the job, as I only ever did "voice acting" when I was a kid, and that was on a cassette recorder, when I was, you know… just goofing around pretending to be a DJ.

Veronese: What was the voice acting and recording process like?

Kaniuga: It was the most fun I have ever had in

Final Fight Streetwise™ Concept Art

my career, but it sure didn't start out that way. I was very nervous in my first recording. I was *trying* too hard. As time went on, I was coached a lot by Gerardo Sprigg, who was a phenomenal voice actor and environment artist. We must have re-recorded the entire game about three times, doing multiple takes of each scene. Sometimes my throat would get so torn up from screaming and grunting, and just… doing that "raspy" thing… that I would just lose my voice. We did so many joke reels. It is unfortunate that some of the funniest moments of those voice recording sessions will never be heard, nor seen.

Veronese: Were you a fan of the *Final Fight* series? I spent many a quarter on the original at one of our local arcades.

Kaniuga: I was familiar with it in a cursory manner. In all honesty, I had never played *Final Fight* until I started working on the game. I can imagine so many *Final Fight* fans groaning as they read that. Don't get me wrong, I played a lot of games from that genre. Where I grew up we had *Bad Dudes*, *Double Dragon*, and the *Teenage Mutant Ninja Turtles* arcade beat 'em up, but no *Final Fight* games.

Veronese: You also did some preliminary work for what was to be *Maximo 3*, correct? What was the extent of the work? The *Maximo/Ghouls 'N Ghost* series is one of my favorite franchises. Susumu Matsushita's visuals are great and the storyline always had a funny, upbeat feel to it, especially with *Maximo vs. Army of Zin*, which was written by fellow comics professional Beau Smith.

Kaniuga: We worked for about 5 months on *Maximo 3*. We had a playable town, enemies, and some awesome new moves planned. It was going to be a lot more open world. In the storyline, Maximo

was going to be investigating a cult out in the desert. We all agreed that we wanted a little bit more of a classic *Zelda* feel in this one, but with a bit darker context. Beau Smith did an excellent job with the previous *game, Maximo vs. Army of Zin*, as did the entire team. I really miss those kinds of games. On *Maximo 3*, Matsushita was only really involved as a rough character designer as I understand it, doing only a handful of drawings. I don't think enough credit is given to the guys that built the models, and painted those textures. Anyone who has done any sort of concept art knows that a modeler can not just look at a flat image, two dimensional image and translate it into three dimensions. A concept artist needs to be there to break down the construction of a design with the modeler, including turnarounds, and just mixing ideas up in person.

Veronese: How did you come to be involved with Blizzard Entertainment? What projects have you worked on?

Kaniuga: After we shipped *Final Fight: Streetwise* at Capcom, I was really interested in working on something heavily stylized. I wanted to work on a fantasy or sci-fi game. I sent my portfolio to my top three developer choices, which were Retro, Double Fine, and Blizzard. Of those three, Blizzard called me back and I did the whole test and interview process. At that time, a lot of people had left Blizzard. They had a total of about 60 developers back in 2006. To give perspective, we now have over 250 developers at Blizzard. I was hired to ignite some fresh new ideas into *The Burning Crusade*, the first expansion to *World of Warcraft*. We churned out the project quite fast, and the team grew just as rapidly. Near the middle of development on *The Wrath of the Lich King*, I was presented with an opportunity to contribute to the

redesign of the art style for *Diablo III*. *Diablo III* had been in development for some time, but the project needed to be reworked. I've been working on it for the past three years, designing many environments and armor sets alongside some of the most talented artists I have ever seen.

Veronese: What is a typical day like for you at Blizzard?

This Page:
Diablo III concept art

Opposite:
CreeD color sketch

Kaniuga: I like to wake up to 1970s disco. While still in a half-dreaming state, I pop up vertically from my bed, and as if I'm in an Old

Spice commercial, then suddenly I'm in the shower saying "Hello ladies." Arriving at work, Matt, the valet guy, takes care of my ride, so I'm not any later than I already am. I like to come in at 10:05 or 10:07, just to, you know, show them that they don't *own* me. But I'm consistent about it so at least they know what to expect.

I drink a Diet Cherry Coke, or a Diet Dr. Pepper, check the mail, and get caught up. I usually have a list of tasks that have to get done, but that's not all I usually do. Throughout the day, I'm usually involved in a slew of meetings, or helping other artists with ideas and critique, as well as facilitating communication between departments. Concept artists have the advantage of working with every art department, so I usually know what

most people are working on. I think we all have a very supportive attitude. The *Diablo III* development process has never been as efficient or enjoyable as it is now. Throughout the day, I forward jpeg files of my sketches and progress to the appropriate managers, work out designs with my co-workers to suit their criteria for a certain feature or model, and share a decent amount of YouTube videos featuring drunk girls at parties that tend to fall over, or dumb kids smashing bikes into trash cans. Our art team shares and studies a LOT of artwork from other studios. Maybe a part of me works in video games so that I can get away with playing them in my free time as "research." I usually don't work more than 9-10 hours a day, and Blizzard asks that we do not work on weekends unless it is *really* necessary. It is probably one of the best gigs in the industry.

Veronese: Is there a dream video game project out there for you? Was there ever a *CreeD* game in the works? I would think *CreeD* would translate really well into a colorful, two dimensional RPG like Earthbound.

Kaniuga: There *was* a *CreeD* video game in development! In 2002 I was working with a small startup studio (made up of former Blizzard employees, ironically) making a Game Boy Advance RPG for *CreeD*. We prototyped it, to the point that *CreeD* could make it rain, alter tiles to flood areas, and modify the dream world with some simple particles. It was quite impressive! But as I moved away from making comics and into games, the brand recognition of *CreeD* began to fade as issues were not coming out regularly. The studio got a pile of money to make something else, and *CreeD* was shelved as a game. Perhaps the new re-release of

CreeD as a collected omnibus will spark new interest in the series, and start a new video game project for the franchise. Of all of my dream projects, I would either like to make a fully painted *Metroid* graphic novel, create a 2.5D side scroller action RPG with a small development team, or work on a *Legend of Zelda* game. When I created *CreeD*, I really wanted it to be a lot like a *Final Fantasy* style world, or something like *Earthbound*. Maybe there is still a chance that that could happen as a game someday.

Veronese: Do you do your concept work using traditional pen and paper or with a tablet? Is concept work typically 2D? Have you done any 3-D modeling or texture work recently or do you typically work with modelers?

Kaniuga: I try to change my process often, just to keep excited and challenge myself with new tools. Sometimes I will do a three-month stretch where I am just sketching on paper, scan it, and Photoshop it afterwards, and then sometimes I will go through a stretch where I do an entire piece using only a computer. I like checking out new software, and what each package is capable of doing. Most concept art is done in 2D, and generally it is very sketchy and quick, and often not even very pretty. The idea is to show the actual construction or functionality of the design or idea. If a modeler can not understand how to build what you are drawing, then it is not good concept art. I have done some modeling and texturing, and it is a much slower process. When doing concept art, you are usually coming up with *tons* of ideas, like every hour of the day. Switching to modeling mode is too slow for me after I have been doing concept work for a while. I

*Left &
Below Left:
World of
Warcraft:
The Burning
Crusade
art*

*Below
Right:
World of
Warcraft:
The Burning
screenshot*

*Opposite:
Nova
Colony*

typically work with several modelers at once, and I ask them about what they would like to see. It is really a collaborative process. My job is to get them stoked about what they are going to be building, and just give them rough guidelines. Enough that they can then add their own creative flair and make it personal for themselves so that they can be proud of the work.

Veronese: Blizzard seems to have the right idea from a creative perspective—enjoy your work, but take a break from it and come back refreshed. Is this a different approach from what some of your colleagues at other companies experience? Do you all go through a "Crunch Time" prior to release that seems to be common in the video game industry? If so, what's that like?

Kaniuga: Most companies can't really afford to spend the kind of time that Blizzard does. I would say that a large percentage of my friends at other companies are doing fifty to sixty hour weeks. On *Diablo III*, our producers understand that people will burn out if they get pushed too hard. Blizzard is really one of the only game studios where they hardly ever ask us to do overtime. However, once we do get into the final few months of a project, most of us voluntarily work longer hours just to get those extra delicious features into the game. I think that level of passion is what makes Blizzard games excel.

Veronese: What video games do you play in your spare time? Are you a console gamer or a PC gamer? What are some of your favorite video games?

Kaniuga: I can't imagine that many people would care about this part of the interview. Hah! But since you asked, I am a big *Metal Gear Solid* junkie. I recruited a bunch of the guys at work in to playing *Metal Gear Solid: Peace Walker* on the PSP. *Metal Gear Solid* is one of the few series that I still go back and play all the time. I usually have a pile of games still in the shrinkwrap, because I just don't have enough time to play them. I usually come home and draw, or socialize. When I can though, I love role-playing games, like the older *Final Fantasy* type RPGs. I like a lot of nonlinear exploration. *Fallout 3*, *Grand Theft Auto 4*, the *Metroid* series, *Legend of Zelda*, *Left 4 Dead*—I try to play everything if only for a bit. I miss the early 2000 era of games. I miss platformers and RPGs with a world map.

Veronese: What's your favorite moment in a video game you've played?

Kaniuga: When the Great Mighty Poo sings that opera song... I wish they would make another *Conker* game.

Veronese: What has it been like to revisit your CreeD work in putting together the *CreeD Omnibus*?

Kaniuga: Honestly, re-mastering and reading all of the old *CreeD* stuff breaks my heart a bit. There is nothing on this planet that I would love to do more than make *CreeD* comics for a living. But I have also changed so dramatically as a person from when I was seventeen and first started publishing *CreeD*. I had always approached *CreeD* somewhat like a journal. It was stuffed with symbols from my own personal journey to understand other people and myself. I had some idea of where I wanted to take the story, but like any real life soul searching journey, it takes time to figure out where the journey is going to go. By the time I knew where to take it, there were so many obstacles—the *CreeD* comic always had the dice loaded against it. I dealt with shady contracts, secret print runs, and scam artists. I made a *lot* of money for a lot of other people.

I scoured the comics business to find a publisher that I could trust, and that would handle the *CreeD Omnibus* with integrity. I found what I believe to be

the right people to do it. And I am going to leave this statement unfinished as it is way too exciting, and you are rather sneaky in how you kind of got me to almost confess something there.

Veronese: Could you tell us a bit about *Nova Colony*?

Kaniuga: *Nova Colony* is a "sci-fi non-romantic comedy" about how love sucks, even in space. The basic premise is that a bunch of scientists put together a space station set in the 1950s, and packed it full of "wholesome" type families, because the Earth's culture was all messed up. Nova is a 19-year-old unemployed kid with a crush, but he has serious issues with understanding women. His bizarre attempts to charm the girl of his dreams usually cause bodily harm to everyone around him, and ultimately destroy any chances he may have ever had with her.

Nova Colony is *very* different from *CreeD*, and for now its just a self-published 48-page book. I worked with Jimm Showman, who wrote an issue of *Scud: Tales from the Vending Machine* with me years ago. With a few other friends we put together three web episodes of *Nova Colony* on YouTube, but adding sound and animation turned out to be *way* too much work for just a couple of dudes to do in our free time as a side project. So we went back to doing a comic book and a few comic strips. Everything about *Nova Colony* is just light-hearted ridiculous fun, and it has been a pleasure to work on.

Veronese: Does you current schedule give you much time to work on comics?

Kaniuga: I pretty much only sleep about five and half hours a night, except for weekends, *but I can't stop!* I only wish I could draw faster. I can't help still making comics in my free time, as it is really, truly a personal expression. When I get letters from people, it means so much to me, just to open that door of communication to people all over the world. It is very rewarding to finish a comic book, and hear the response, as it gives me a sense of purpose, like I am leaving some kind of mark, even if only a handful of people were listening. I don't think I'll ever be able to stop.

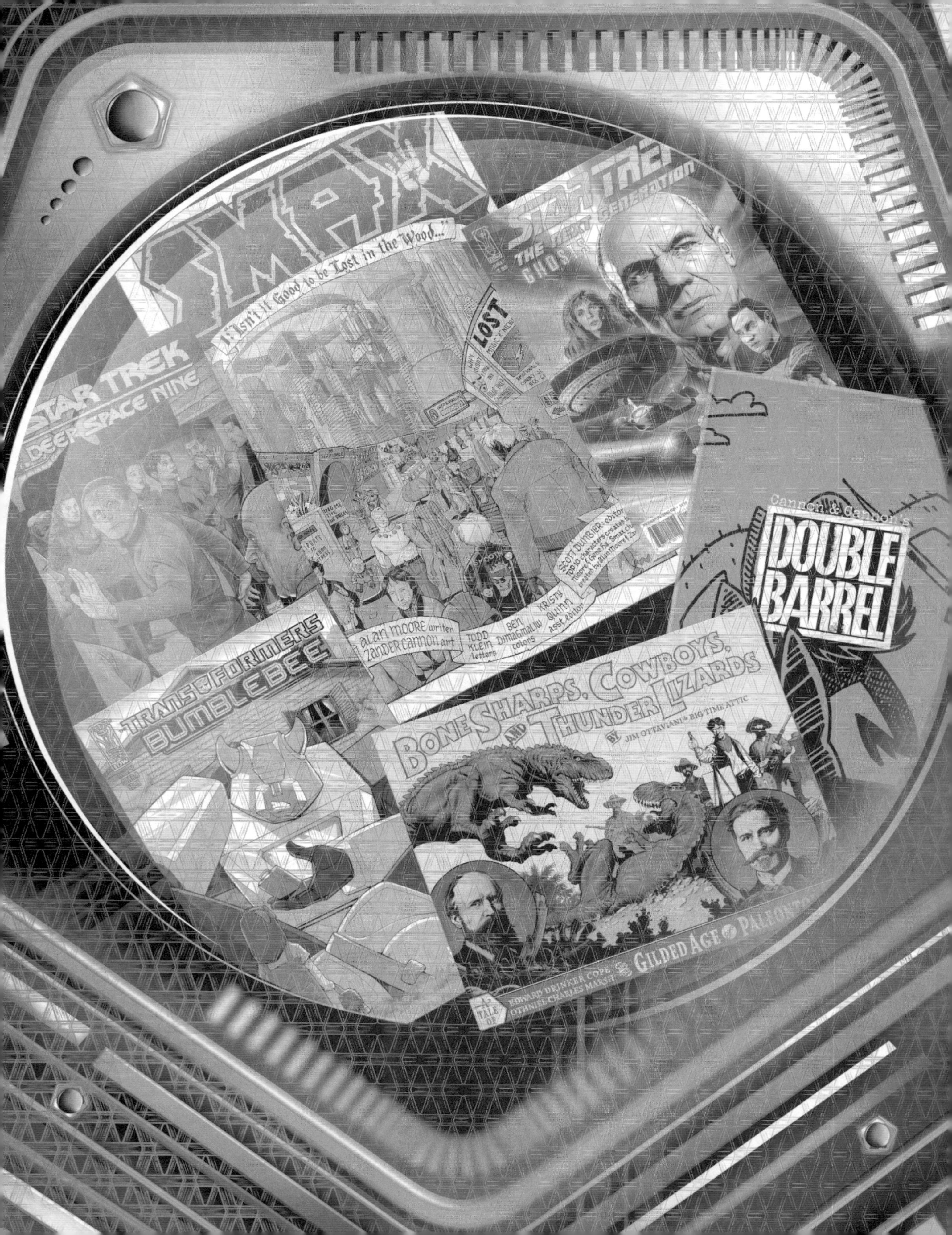
STAR TREK
DEEP SPACE NINE
"Isn't it Good to be Lost in the Wood..."
LOST
ALAN MOORE writer
ZANDER CANNON art
TODD KLEIN letters
BEN DIMAGMALIW colors
KRISTY QUINN asst. editor
SCOTT DUNBIER editor
STAR TREK THE NEXT GENERATION
Cannon & Cannon's
DOUBLE BARREL
TRANSFORMERS
BUMBLEBEE
BONE SHARPS, COWBOYS, AND THUNDER LIZARDS
BY JIM OTTAVIANI & BIG TIME ATTIC
A TALE OF
EDWARD DRINKER COPE
OTHNIEL CHARLES MARSH

Zander**Cannon**

Zander Cannon is probably best known in comic book circles for his hyper-detailed artwork on Alan Moore's *Top 10*. *Top 10* that tells the story of a superhero police force handling day-to-day problems in Neopolis, a city where everyone has super powers. Over the years, Cannon has become involved with creating graphic novels about factual science subjects. Cannon and long-time collaborator Kevin Cannon (no relation) make up the studio Big Time Attic, with the duo frequently collaborating on these projects.

The majority of Zander's current work aims to communicate an understanding of biology and biochemistry with humor and ease in graphic novel form. *The Stuff of Life: A Graphic Guide to Genetics and DNA* and *Evolution: The Story of Life on Earth* provide an excellent foundation on both subjects for a student of any level, while maintaining an accessible entry point. The star of these books is the crown prince of Glargal, a sea cucumber-like alien, who is being taught about life on other planets. Zander has tackled quarrels between scoundrel paleontologists in *Bone Sharps, Cowboys, and Thunder Lizards*, and a look at the history of the space race in *T-Minus: The Race to the Moon*. Zander is a video game fan, one that plays an interesting role though an annual contribution he makes to the video game magazine, *Game Informer*, a magazine with a phenomenal average circulation of eight million copies a month.

Opposite: (l to r)
Star Trek: Deep Space Nine #2, Top Ten #8 interior page, Star Trek: The Next Generation Ghosts #1, Transformers: Bumblebee #4, Bone Sharps, Cowboys, and Thunder Lizards and Double Barrel #1

Above:
The Stuff of Life

Keith Veronese: How were you approached by the magazine *Game Informer*?

Zander Cannon: I met a former editor of *Game Informer*, Jeremy Zoss, through a mutual friend at San Diego Comic-Con, and I believe he had seen some of my stuff before. The funny thing about meeting Jeremy in San Diego was that Jeremy and I and the mutual friend (Pat Gleason), not to mention *Game Informer* itself, are all in the Twin Cities in Minnesota, within twenty minutes travel time of each other.

I believe they were looking at changing artists on *Game Infarcer* because they wanted something a little more "realistic," which is not really my forte. I believe what they were looking for was something a little more dynamic and less like a gag cartoon. I think what clinched it was when we all sat down for the first one, a joke preview of the then-unreleased *Halo 3*. We were playing on people's inflated expectations for the game, the first *Halo* game released on the Xbox 360, so I took the *Game Informer* staff's dozen or so jokes and added about a dozen of my own, as well as homages to old video games and so forth. Piling a ton of references and jokes into one illustration is one of my favorite things to do, and I think the fact that I was savvy about games, game culture, and *Halo* in particular let the people at *Game Informer* know that I was the man for the job.

Veronese: Your work on the *Halo 3* image is amazing, your detail-oriented style worked very well for it. I don't think there was a genre of games not covered in the image—you included everything from cart racing to sports to puzzle games. The cover really fits the outlandish set of video

game fan expectations at the time. As someone who waited in line for 4 hours for the game, I can tell you that video game fan expectations are every bit as high as those of comic book fans, and maybe higher. What's your favorite inside joke in the *Halo 3* piece? Did you have high expectations for *Halo 3* at the time?

Cannon: I can actually answer both questions at the same time. I did have extremely high expectations for *Halo 3*, but in the months before the release of *Halo 2*, I was going nuts. I read any and all bits of information relating to the game, and one of the things I thought was kind of funny was that one of the people at Bungie, maybe Jason Jones, said that *Halo 2* was *Halo*, except on fire, going ninety miles per hour through a hospital zone, and being chased by ninjas. And the ninjas are also on fire. So when I was drawing the *Halo 3* image, I thought I'd put in a ninja on fire for the three people who read that same blurb by Jason Jones two years before.

Veronese: Your "easter egg" style as seen on *Top 10* and other comic titles suits the work you've done for *Game Informer* well, especially their "tongue in cheek" April Fool's issue.

What has been your favorite piece so far that you contributed to *Game Informer*?

Above:
Halo 3 parody art

Left:
Bioshock 2 parody art

Opposite: (top to bottom)
Sacred Cow Barbecue art created for *Game Informer*

Cannon: My favorite piece was probably the most recent one, for the currently nonexistent *Bioshock 3*, both because it's the most sophisticated artistically and because its references are pretty consistently funny. I kept checking in with the editors there and showing them the drawing at every stage, so I got a lot of additional feedback, and there are a couple jokes that they thought of when they saw sketches that I would never have thought of.

Veronese: *The Game Infarcer Bioshock 3* cover is a great piece of work. It is almost believable within the realm of the series in the way it shows character progression from Big Brother to Little Sister to Big Grandfather. I love the interjection of the "Ryan's Buffet" service counter, the Seven Day Pill Box on the Big Grandfather's back, and the Ayn Rand references. What were some references that the editorial staff put in?

Cannon: The meeting we had involved maybe a half-dozen editors and myself, and together we came up with most of the main jokes that have to do with both old people and the *Bioshock* world. Joe Juba, one of the editors there, really wanted the Android Ryan joke in there, and we were trying to figure out a way to put in a golf club. I think I came up with the pill box thing, someone there suggested the big fiber supplement valve, that sort of thing. That kind of brainstorming meeting is really fun, especially because everyone knows that I'm going to filter through everything when I sit down to draw it, so they know they can say anything, no matter how crazy.

Also, and this happens pretty often, when the drawing was almost done, I had put in a sign at the host stand that just said "Please wait to be seated". When I sent it in to the editors at *Game Informer*, Jeff Cork pointed out that it really should say "Would you kindly wait to be seated." It's one of those things that I totally should have thought of, as it fits the game better, but you get so involved in drawing the picture that sometimes things get past you.

The only other illustrations I did were for some articles called *Sacred Cow Barbecue* in which the editors basically talked about how classic games were not really all that good, That was fun, as I got to draw each of the games being destroyed in some way or another. But like the *Game Infarcer* covers, they are for games that have been out for a very long time.

Veronese: *Game Informer* has an average circulation of roughly forty times that of the highest selling comic book, with *Game Informer* having a circulation of nearly 8 million. How does it feel to be the torch bearer and a connection to comics for such a large audience?

Cannon: I guess I never thought of it that way. I'd say that the connection to comics is pretty thin, since the *Game Infarcer* illustrations aren't comics themselves, but it is nice that they choose to have art for it that is done in a fairly low-tech, ink-on-paper style; essentially a comic book style. It is a nice contrast when practically everything else in the magazine is 3-D rendered, high-dynamic-range imagery.

Veronese: You mentioned you were a consistent

video game player. Are you a console or PC gamer?

Cannon: I'm a console gamer, mostly because the computers I use are also for work, so it is not a good idea for me to have games on them. Right now I have an Xbox 360, a PS2, and a DS. I will probably get a PS3 soon so I can play *God of War 3*, *Heavy Rain*, and *Uncharted 2*.

Veronese: So you are definitely gamer. What are your three favorite games of all time?

Cannon: It's hard to whittle down my list of all-time favorite games, but the first two *Oddworld games*, *Portal*, and *Batman: Arkham Asylum* are up there and *Shadow of the Colossus*, too. Oh, and *Knights of the Old Republic* and the *Katamari* games.

Veronese: *Batman: Arkham Asylum* was a coup, showing that a licensed comic book game could actually be the "Game of the Year." Bruce Timm worked on that game as well, with his work showing in the quality and the mood. Since you're a video game player, would you want to cast a vote for the worst comic book video game?

Cannon: I don't know about worst, since I know there are some really terrible ones out there, but *Batman: The Caped Crusader* for the Amiga (1988) was the hardest on me personally. It looked great and it played like a pretty standard platform game with RPG elements. The problem was, however, that your character (Batman, of course) was constantly losing health and you had to eat or heal yourself constantly in order not to drop dead at any moment from the sheer horror of being Batman. Even when I would play the game as cautiously as I could and switch to my inventory screen, the only place where the player could tell how close you were to death, with ludicrous frequency, I would just walk into a room, get in a short battle with the Joker or whoever else was waiting, and just suddenly die. And then when that happened, I just started again at the beginning, over and over again.

Veronese: Do you have any interest in working directly on a video game project in the future? Any dream projects out there that you would like to work on?

Cannon: I'd love to work on a video game project. There have been several near misses for me in terms

of working on comic book adaptations of video games, but nothing strictly in the video game industry *per se*. A dream project, I suppose, would be to be involved with a game as not just a writer or artist, but someone who looks at the interactivity of the project, looking at how to manage conversation trees and how to allow the player to complete the game in their own style. Something large scale.

Veronese: Speaking of your interest in *Heavy Rain* and your desire to work on conversation trees and open-ended game play, where do you see video games going in the next 5 to 10 years? It seems like BioWare and a couple other companies have set the standard for the merged "Action-RPG." Are there any comic properties that you think would fit this style of game?

Cannon: My great hope is that the type of games where you basically choose the dark side or the light side like the BioWare games would become less about simply being good or bad and become more of a spectrum—more about having a personal playing style. It's all too easy to simply choose the good option and take the good path. But what if always doing the nicest thing would attract non-player characters that would take advantage of you and waste your time? Or even keep you away from people who really did need your help? Then you would have to start really thinking about what people are asking and try to find the sweet spot where you're doing good things, and avoid being a sucker. The same sort of result goes along with being a "bad" character in those games. If you are too bad, you'll get locked out of certain quests or areas until you work things out.

The main thing here is not about branching paths and multiple play-throughs, but playing style. I was really proud that in the first *Mass Effect* I maxed out my persuasion skills very early on so I accomplished a lot of goals in the game with no fighting. I was disappointed to see that gone in *Mass Effect 2*, where you earn persuasion abilities from just sticking hard to the good or bad path, which to me is a step back in gameplay.

Also, I really like open-world games in which you can wander around and get missions. I like the idea that those games would increase in density, so that you wouldn't have to check the map as much, but rather find missions just by looking around and recognizing patterns. I love *Grand Theft Auto 4* and *Just Cause 2* for slightly different reasons, but I really wouldn't mind a much smaller world that had more of a focus on exploration and finding clues in the environment than on roaring twenty miles across a map for a mission.

Veronese: What is your working relationship with Kevin Cannon like? Has Kevin worked on any video game projects? Was he involved with any of the *Game Infarcer* work?

Cannon: Kevin and I work together on educational comics for book publishers and other collaborative long-term projects, but single illustrations are frequently done independently of each other, as it is usually only one image we are working on for *Game Infarcer* and they are typically relatively simple. Also, when a new one comes in, Kevin typically asks me if it has anything to do with *Goldeneye* for the Nintendo 64. If not, he's not interested.

Veronese: The first *Top 10* series (1999, Wildstorm/ABC comics) features several video game references, particularly in issue 8, which clearly shows the protagonist in Williams Entertainment's *Joust* in the background, the side-story about the release of the *Top 10* video game, and (possibly) the invention of the Ipad (I think Steve Jobs owes Gene Ha, Alan Moore, and yourself some amount of residuals). Were you responsible for a lot of the "extras" and pop culture references in the background?

Cannon: On the original run of *Top 10*, I probably contributed a quarter to a third of the jokes in the background, but all of the video game stuff you mention was either Alan Moore or Gene Ha. I put some video game references in *Smax* and the new seasons of *Top 10*. The *Portal* Companion Cube makes an appearance in an upcoming issue.

Veronese: If the *Top 10* series was steeped in the world of *The Wire/NYPD Blue*, the follow-up limited series, *Smax*, was set in a world of *Lord of the Rings*-

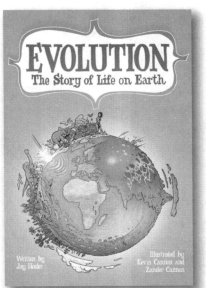

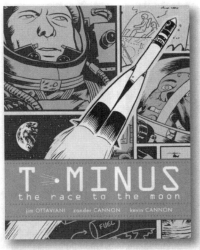

esque mythology, fairy tales, and role-playing games. The story (and your art) for the series has a "dungeon crawler" feel, even including minimum requirements for a party, fulfilling a series of side-quests before embarking on the main quest, and attaining mystical weapons. A lot of these aspects are probably literary references, but video games could also be said to be the predominant medium wherein this type of story is currently told (for example, most people my age know the story of Aeris dying in *Final Fantasy VII*, the basic story of *Chrono Trigger*, etc.) Was a leaning to this type of storytelling, either in the script or the art, intentional?

Cannon: I would say that that stuff was largely more about *Lord of the Rings* and *Harry Potter* and other literary or cinematic work rather than video games. I don't think Alan Moore is much of a gamer, and any contributions I had toward what you're talking about would be mostly background jokes or character designs. I'm sure that paper role-playing games had a significant impact on the tone, but it's probably more influenced by the things that also influenced fantasy video games than it is by video games themselves.

Veronese: What do the next couple of years hold for you projectwise?

Cannon: What's next are big years in educational comics for us. We're working on a college textbook in graphic novel form, and we've got another younger readers science book coming out, *Evolution: The Story of Life on Earth*.

[**Author's note:** *If you haven't read Cannon's previous science-related work,* T-Minus: The Race to the Moon, *is a spectacular example that chronologically details the ups and downs of the Soviet and U.S. attempts to put a human on the moon.*] More *Top 10* comics are on the way from DC/Wildstorm as well, and a few other science-fiction projects that are starting up.

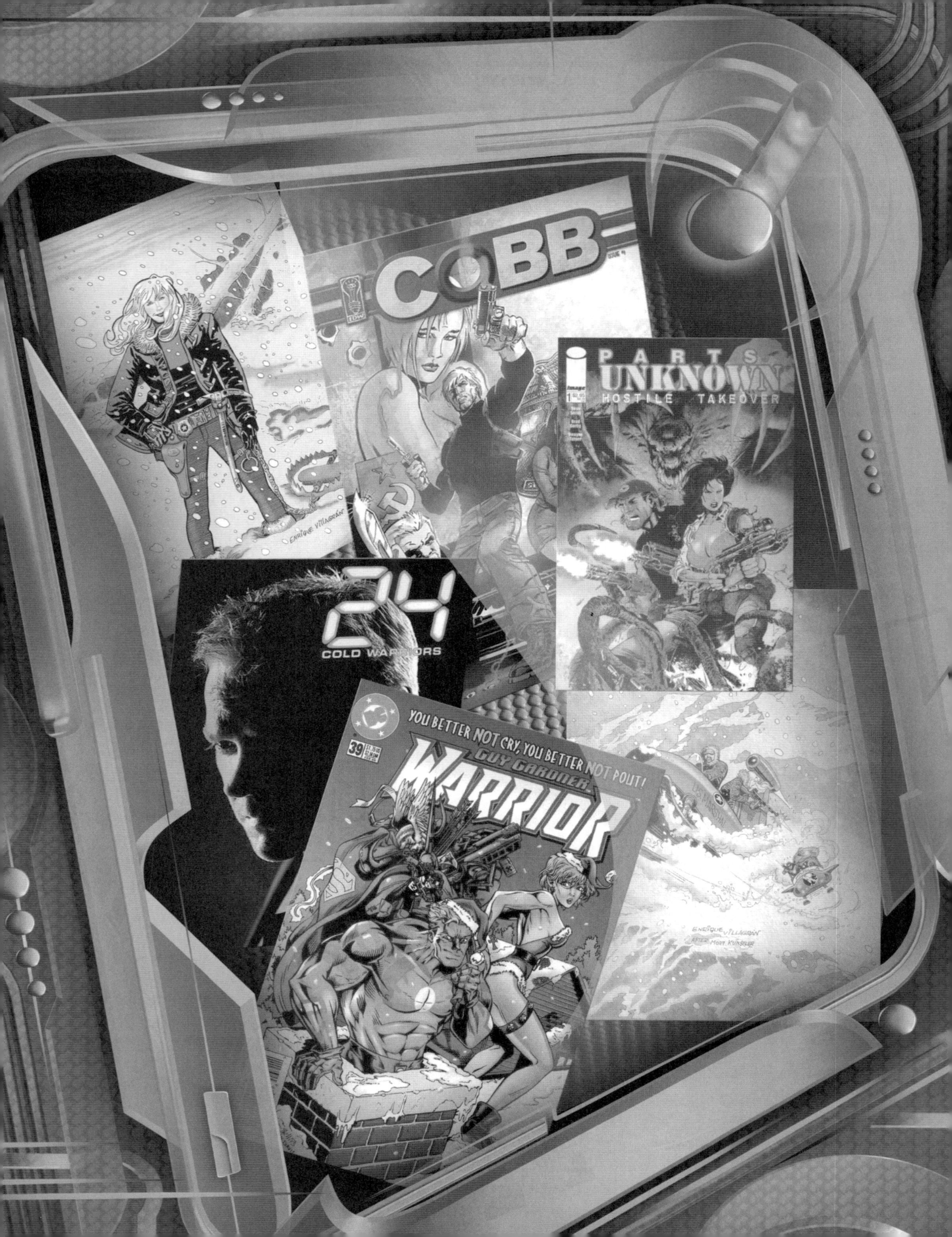
ENRIQUE VILLAGRÁN
COBB
PARTS UNKNOWN
HOSTILE TAKEOVER
24
COLD WARRIORS
YOU BETTER NOT CRY, YOU BETTER NOT POUT!
39
GUY GARDNER
WARRIOR
ENRIQUE VILLAGRÁN
AFTER MORT KUNSTLER

Beau**Smith**

Beau Smith has worked as a writer and columnist for numerous companies, including DC Comics, Image Comics, the now defunct Eclipse Comics, and IDW Publishing. During his tenure at Image Comics, Beau oversaw much of the *Spawn* line, and while at IDW, he helped supply some of Jack Bauer's backstory through the one-shot *24: Cold Warriors*. Smith is probably best known for his work on *Guy Gardner: Warrior*, where he helped turn the former Green Lantern Guy Gardner into a walking instrument of mass destruction, keeping the tone light and funny along the way. While working in comics, Beau worked on a number of video game projects, which we will talk about extensively. Beau Smith is also working on three creator-owned comics at the moment—*Wynonna Earp*, *Parts Unknown*, and *Cobb*.

Keith Veronese: The *Maximo* series takes place in the same universe as the terribly difficult, but classic 1980s Capcom title, *Ghouls 'N Ghosts*. Were you familiar with *Ghouls 'N Ghosts*? If so, had you played it?

Beau Smith: No, I wasn't. I had heard through a lot of my game playing buddies that *Ghouls 'N Ghosts* was a pretty hard game to crack. Capcom gave me plenty of background material on it and that helped me a great deal in getting the lay of the land.

Veronese: *Maximo vs. Army of Zin* is considered by many to be one of the best games to come out for the PlayStation 2 (which says a lot, as there were over 3,000 games that came out for the platform). How did you come to be involved in the project?

Opposite: (clockwise0
Wynonna #1, Cobb #1, Parts Unknown #1, Wynonna #2, Guy Gardner: Warrior #39, and 24: Cold Warriors #1

Above:
Ghost 'N Goblins packaging and screenshot

Beau Smith: Originally, Scott Rogers, who was in charge of rounding up talent for this project with Capcom, called on my good friend and sometimes comic book writing partner, Chuck Dixon, (*G.I. Joe, Batman, Conan*) to see if he was interested in writing *Maximo vs. Army Of Zin.* Chuck's schedule at the time was full up with his writing at DC Comics and a million other places. Chuck suggested my name to Scott. So, Scott called me up and asked me if I was interested in writing it. I said, "Sure!" I'm always looking for a chance to widen my writing resume and I had never written a video game at that point.

Scott told me that they needed the story written in screenplay format and that was no problem for me. Capcom was reaching out to comic book writers because they wanted more depth in the characters though their dialogue and story pacing. They were looking to break away from the standard storytelling style that video games were in at that point.

Veronese: It is really refreshing that Capcom brought in specific talent to flesh out the characters and dialogue. A lot of times, especially with games initially produced for the Japanese market, North American and European gamers are left with crude and sometimes funny translations. One that immediately comes to mind is the "Jill, Master of Unlocking Things" line immortalized in the first *Resident Evil* game. Do you know of any other projects that Capcom specifically was seeking outside talent for during this time period?

Beau Smith: Nope. I had to sign a bunch of "Top Secret" papers when I began work on the project, so they kept everything "*Maximo* Only" on our dealings.

Veronese: What was the extent that you worked on *Maximo vs. Army of Zin?*

Beau Smith: I wrote none of the "game action." Capcom and their designers had all that worked out.

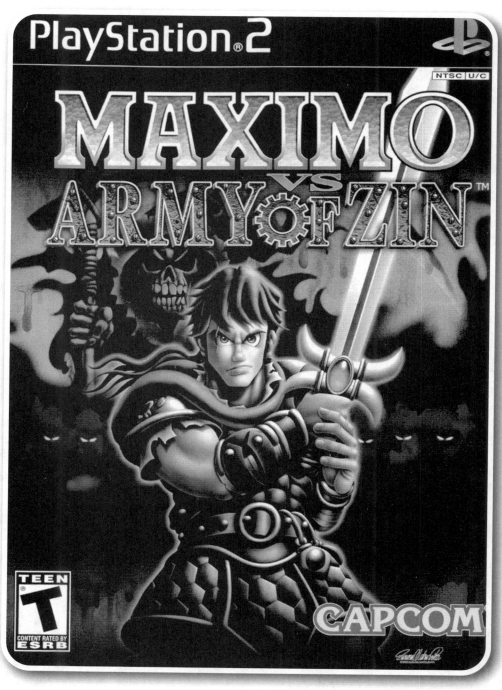

I was there to make up the story and give the characters life through dialogue and story pacing. It was like writing the movie within the movie. Point A to Point B was already dictated in the game play. I was there to give it character life. Through dialogue I got to give each character their own distinct personality and voice. I also did my best to add a sense of humor to them. At that point I felt that was something lacking in a lot of video game characters.

Veronese: What was the script outline for *Maximo vs. Army of Zin* like since the gameplay was laid out?

Beau Smith: I wrote it in screenplay format from my own head. They had given me some Point A to

Point B direction as far as where the game play was gonna go, but again, I was surprised at how much freedom they gave me with the characters and the story. They were a great bunch to work for.

Veronese: I see a lot of your humor in the character of Grimm—am I right? Did you write the dialogue for when Maximo interacts with villagers? I seem to remember a "Do you need a sidekick?" line" that sounds like you as well?

Beau Smith: Yeah, as a writer, I strongly believe that you need to add layers of humanizing, likeable ways to all characters, be they good or bad. It's what makes them "real" to the reader or viewer. A story without any sense of humor is never as compelling. Grimm was a blast to write because since he was "Death" and had seen everything, I thought he should have a real dark humor about him and is always amused by those that haven't seen everything yet. I also wanted to show a true friendship between Grimm and Maximo. Lord knows with the lives they've both lead, they could use a friend. I wrote Maximo as a world-weary warrior and somewhat grouchy. Grimm was always there to balance out Maximo's darker moments and keep him from being totally dark, which he could be if left unattended. Grimm realizes this and makes sure he is always there to back his warrior buddy up.

Veronese: Were there any story elements from *Maximo vs. Army of Zin* that you really like that didn't make it into the final game? What was your favorite part that you wrote?

Beau Smith: My favorite parts were the scenes with Grimm and Maximo. I enjoyed writing their buddy relationship and dialogue. They were my *Lethal Weapon* and *Butch Cassidy and the Sundance Kid* moments. Those parts still make me smile when I force someone to play the game and let me watch. There were all kinds of bits and pieces that got left out just due to time and space. I had some nice romantic scenes that I hated to lose as well as slobberknocking fight scenes that I wish there was more time for.

Veronese: The *Maximo* series features art by the Manga artist Susumu Matsushita, whose style is known for its Western influences (a reverse Joe Madureira if you will). Were you familiar with Matsushita's art prior to working on *Maximo vs. Army of Zin*?

Beau Smith: No, I wasn't. I have to be very honest with you, the last video games that I ever played were *Pong* and *Pac Man*. I was pretty terrible at them even then. I haven't played one since. So as far as my actual knowledge of games, I was pretty much a newbie. After I got involved with *Maximo* I did become familiar with the work of Matsushita and was knocked out with the work. The storyboard and model sheets that Capcom provided me were amazing. It really stoked my desire to make this the best work I could.

Veronese: What were you provided with by Capcom in regards to backstory and art design by Capcom prior to starting on *Maximo vs. Army of Zin*? Did you get to see an early version of the game?

Beau Smith: I didn't see any early

Opposite:
Maximo vs. Army of Zin packaging

Above:
Maximo

Left:
Maximo vs. Army of Zin screenshot

version of the game, but they did send me tons of sketches and model sheets that I was sworn to secrecy on. Most of what I was provided with was given to me via our phone conversations where again, I was the one doing most of the talking about story and characters. They really let me fly on this and as a writer, you can't ask for more.

Veronese: Have you worked on any other video game projects? Were you involved in any never materialized?

Beau Smith: I've worked on pitches for video games based on my own comic book properties such as *Wynonna Earp* and *Parts Unknown*, but nothing materialized as of yet. While working for Todd McFarlane Productions I got to dip my writing hand in a few things there of Todd's properties, but nothing that put me on the credits.

Veronese: *Wynonna Earp* is a comic screaming for a video game to be made of it—it's almost the perfect material for a game. It has a solid backstory (relative of Wyatt Earp), trailer-trash vampires, mafia mummies, and would make for a great first- or third-person shooter. *Cobb* would work extremely well too (and even though it's not creator-owned, I would purchase a *Guy Gardner: Warrior* game in a heartbeat). How did you go about pitching *Wynonna Earp* and *Parts Unknown* to video game companies? What is the pitch process like for creator-owned properties?

Beau Smith: When *Wynonna Earp* was first released as a comic through Image Comics/Wildstorm, I, along with Ted Adams and Kris Oprisko of then Wildstorm, now of IDW Publishing, had a pitch meeting with a video company from Japan. I have to say in all good humor, it was one of the worst pitch meetings I ever had. At that time we were lacking experience, and the chemistry with the video game company just didn't click. I felt I didn't

describe *Wynonna Earp* well enough to them. Funny now, but not so much then, I left the meeting feeling pretty lost. The language barrier didn't help much either. I felt bad for Ted and Kris at Wildstorm. I always felt I kinda let them down on that. Currently IDW is talking to people about a *Wynonna Earp* video game and it comes at a time when *Wynonna Earp: The Yeti Wars* and *The Complete Wynonna Earp* trade paperback will be released. Ted and IDW are one of the most successful publishers out there and I think the chances of Wynonna becoming a video game are much better. The same with *Cobb*. *Cobb* is also in IDW's very capable hands. As far as *Parts Unknown*, the screenplay is almost finished right now, and it is being repped by Propeller Productions and Peter LeFevere. He's also talking to some folks about it as a video game as well. I'd love to see all three hit it as games as well as my *Lost and Found* property through IDW. *Guy Gardner: Warrior*—mnn… One day I would love to see DC Comics collect my issues and let me do some stories on his transition from Warrior back to a Green Lantern. I would be so stoked. But, as you mentioned, it's not creator-owned, so the chances of *Guy Gardner: Warrior* ever showing back up are slim right now.

Veronese: What was the extent of your work on the games that came out of Todd McFarlane Productions? Do you remember which games you were involved in? It's not uncommon for a lot of this work to go uncredited.

Beau Smith: Naaaw, with Todd I was mainly doing my job as Executive Director of Marketing and Promotions. By that time, Todd had a ton of specialized folks in that field that he had working on the creative end. To be very honest, Todd handled most of it himself. Nothing concerning

Spawn ever got out without his creative eyes and hands on it.

Veronese: You wrote the *Maximo: Beauty is Only Sword Deep* one-shot from Dreamwave—how did that come about (especially as the one-shot came out two years after *Maximo vs. Army of Zin* was released)? Was this a natural transition of the two genres?

Beau Smith: That came about not only through my work at Capcom, but with Pat Lee of Dreamwave. Pat was the artist on my *Wynonna Earp* series issues #4 and #5 for Image Comics. Pat and I had become very good amigos. When Dreamwave got the rights to do comic books based on some of the Capcom games, with *Maximo* being one of them, Pat called me up and we made the deal in about 10 seconds. I had the best time doing that one-shot. The art on the comic was given special treatment to have the look of the game and Dreamwave even added extra layers and time to the coloring of the book to give it more of a cinematic feel. In the comic book I had just as much creative control as I did with the game. Both Capcom and Dreamwave pretty much let me have at it. It was 95% total creative freedom. They brought me on to give the characters a personal life and that's what I tried to do.

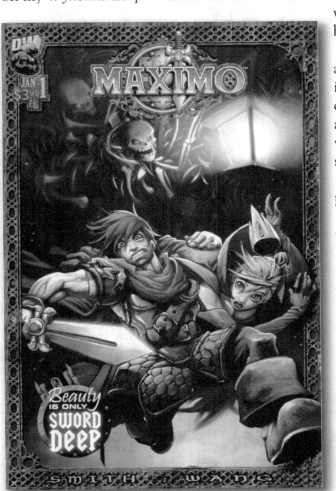

Veronese: Dreamwave did some amazing work printing the issue—the colors, like you said, are very nice, extremely well layered and vibrant. I miss a lot of the comics Dreamwave put out from around that time, especially their *Transformers* line. Were there plans for you to work on any other *Maximo* comics or Capcom properties with Dreamwave?

Beau Smith: Yeah, I was also supposed to do a *Deathstalkers* comic for them, but it didn't happen. I'm not sure where things ended up at that point with it. I was also supposed to do more *Maximo*

stories, but I believe Dreamwave's option on the comics had run out at that point. I was really enjoying the groove of doing *Maximo*, I wish I we could've done more.

Veronese: Any other video game projects planned for the future? Are there any plans for a *Maximo 3*?

Beau Smith: No other games planned right now. I am always open to do more. Like I said before, I really enjoyed it and with games being so much more advanced with stories today, my thrill level in writing another one would be at full throttle.

I haven't heard if there's a *Maximo 3* yet, but if there is, I'd love to revisit the characters. I would love another crack at the war-weary warrior with the big sword.

Veronese: Did you ever play video games regularly?

Beau Smith: As I mentioned earlier, *Pong* was the last game I played. I am so inept when it comes to playing video games. I'm like at chimp at the controls; in fact, a chimp would probably be far superior to me. When *Maximo vs. The Army Of Zin* came out and I got my copies, I had to have my son, Nick, load it up and play it so I could see what I had done. Pretty funny and yet pretty sad at the same time. Nick still busts my chops because I'm so very bad playing video games.

Veronese: You have worn many hats during your career, something that is very admirable.

Beau Smith: Thank you for the kind words, Keith. I've always tried to stay busy on both the business and creative end.

It keeps doughnuts on the table if you're getting a check from everyone.

Opposite:
Wynonna Earp: The Yeti Wars

Above:
Maximo: Beauty is only Sword Deep #1

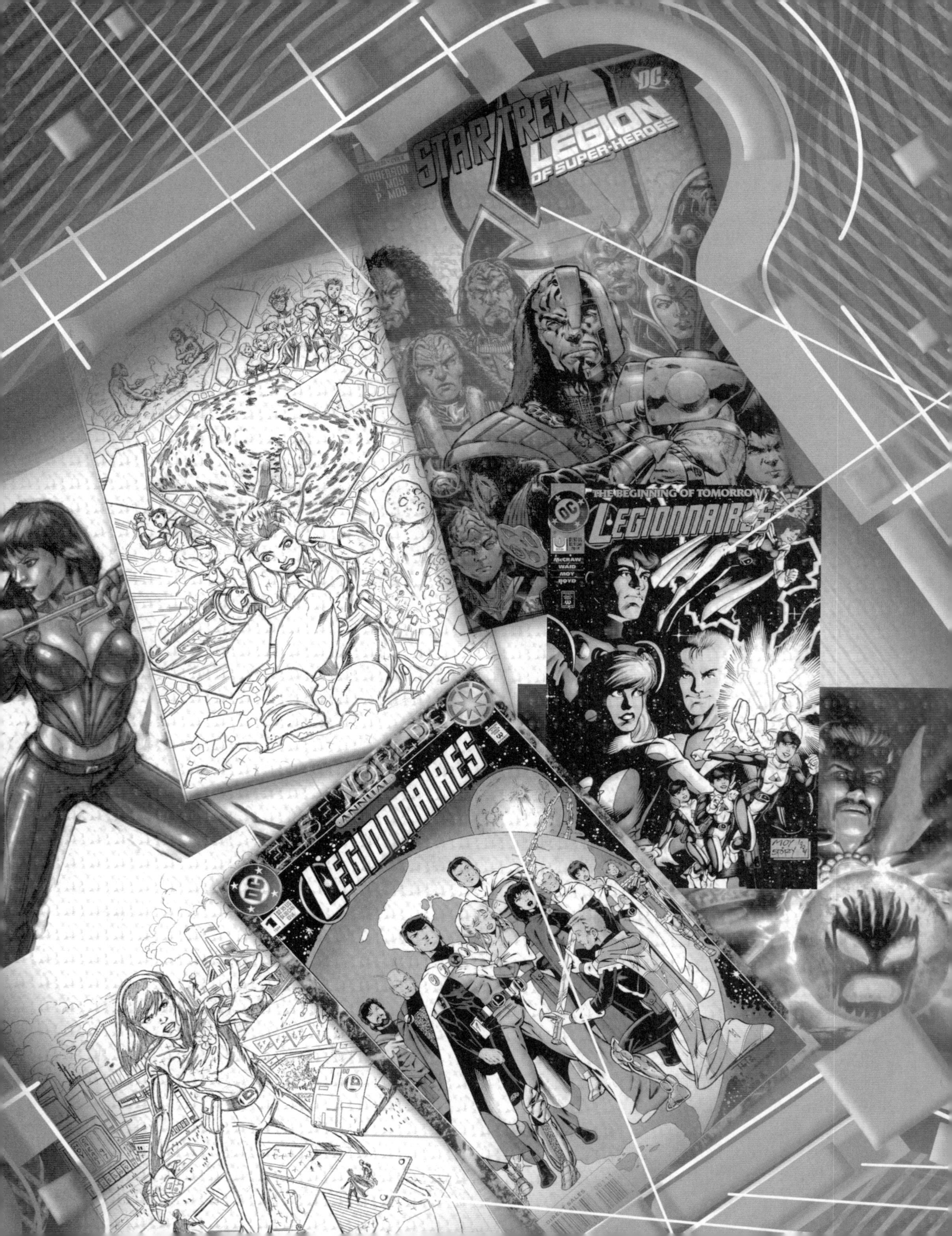

DC
STAR TREK
LEGION OF SUPER-HEROES
ROBERSON
J. MOY
P. MOY
THE BEGINNING OF TOMORROW!
LEGIONNAIRES
McCRAW
WAID
MOY
BOYD
MOY STORY
LEGIONNAIRES
ANNUAL

Jeffrey**Moy**

Jeffrey Moy is best known for his critically acclaimed five-year run on *Legionnaries*, a stretch almost unheard of in modern comics. After his time at DC Comics, Moy pursued a different path, working in character and environment design for several different video game companies. Jeffrey Moy recently returned to the world of comics with the much anticipated *Star Trek/Legion of Super-Heroes* series published by IDW and DC Comics.

Keith Veronese: What was your original career goal? Was it a job in comics?

Jeffrey Moy: Hmm...that one goes back a while. I think I was aiming for storyboarding or doing something in movies, but during college, I focused more on comic storytelling as it seemed more feasible, and at the time, easier for me to get a job doing. I already had some contacts in the comic industry, but I really had no access or information on getting into storyboarding or movies.

Veronese: How did you get involved with Raven Software?

Moy: One of my instructors from Northern Illinois University, Mark Nelson, had ben working at Raven Software for a few years and a bunch of us would go and visit him from time to time as Madison was only two hours from Chicago. We would visit the studio and hang out for a bit. Then it just so happened that I picked up a job to pencil a comic book adaptation of a *Star Trek: Voyager* video game called *Star Trek Voyager: Elite Force* that Wildstorm put out in 2000. That was a cool experience, because I knew the guys that were working on the game. Getting access to reference for characters and environments made the book much easier to work on. After that job, I was looking for work for about six months when I decided it was probably a good time to look for a position that would be more stable. On one visit to Raven I asked the art director, Brian Pelletier, if they were looking to hire anyone with my abilities. It just so happened that

Opposite: (clockwise)
Elektra color art, *Adventure Comics #526* pencils, *Star Trek/Legion of Super-Heroes #3*, *Legionnaires #0*, Dr. Strange color art, *Legionnaires Annual #1*, and *Legionnaires #5* pencils

Above:
Star Trek/Legion of Super-Heroes #1

a project was ramping up and in a month I was hired as an artist for *Star Wars Jedi Knight II: Jedi Outcast.*

Veronese: You are best known for a five-year run on DC's *Legionnaires,* one of the longest runs on the *Legion* family of titles. How does your day-to-day work differ now? What's the single biggest benefit of working in video games?

Moy: Working freelance in comics is great if you have a steady flow of work coming in, but I think that uncertainty always weighs heavily in the back of your mind when you're just jumping from job to job and constantly looking for more work. Working in a studio like Raven takes all that off my shoulders and I can just focus on drawing. My day-to-day in comics was very free and up to me to decide when I needed to work, which as my best friend and choice inker, W. C. Carani, always put as, "Which 12 hours of the day do you want to work?" But honestly, it never felt like work. You just need to be dedicated and discipline yourself to do it.

Working at Raven is much more like a job that most office jobs are like, in the sense that there is a physical building I drive to and there is a cubicle with my name on it. There is administration, a human resource department, some office politics, but I think that's where the similarities end. The environment and people are all very creative and engaged and working as part of a group dedicated to getting a product out the door is just as rewarding as working in comics. I still draw every day, but now I do it on a Cintiq tablet,

which offers me the closest feeling to drawing on paper, and work on creating environmental concepts for designers and set dressers to look at for ideas and inspiration.

The biggest benefit for me in comics is that freedom to work when you want to/feel like it, the enjoyment of telling stories, and having a product out there that you can hold in your hands month after month that other people can enjoy and look forward to your next book.

Raven Software offers stability, benefits, more pay, and I still get to do what I love, which is drawing every day. To me it doesn't matter what I'm drawing, chairs and tables, science labs or hallways, it's all good.

Veronese: What is one of your favorite experiences while working on a video game?

Moy: My first game, *Jedi Knight II: Jedi Outcast* was really a learning experience as well as having my favorite experience. First of all, it's *Star Wars!* How could you beat that for your first game? Then it's just learning about how a game comes together from an idea to everyone working together to push the final product out the door. I think I had a giddy moment when I saw a concept for an automated turret that I had done appear in the game as a fully built, textured, and animated asset. I was blown away. They followed the concept to a "t" and it looked and did exactly what I imagined.

Veronese: How did you add textures work to your repertoire? Do you prefer it to doing concept art or designs?

Moy: As a game progresses, you reach a point where you need less concept work and more production work to be done. When that happens, I shift gears and start doing more texture work. It's a nice change of pace and a bit more procedural now due to changes in how textures are made. We used to paint textures, on one map, but now, you have at least three maps, one for color diffuse, one for specular, one for normals, with this adding the illusion of a 3-D texture onto an object. There are several others maps that can be added, but all of them will be joined in the engine and you will then end up with what you see on the screen. I enjoy doing textures, but for me, concept work is where it's at.

Veronese: Were you experienced with texture or computer graphic editing prior to moving to the video game industry?

Moy: Not at all. I had a little bit of Photoshop experience; I think my brother, Philip, had more before I joined Raven. At the time in 2001, I don't think there were enough people in the industry that specialized in it, so you hire someone that has artistic skill and you train them to learn the tools and process. I consider myself lucky, because nowadays, the video game market is flooded with students coming out of school with game industry degrees and companies are being much more selective and expect the person they hire to have a certain skill set.

Veronese: Has computer graphic work led you to move to penciling using a tablet?

Moy: Not at all. For comic

book work I still love the feel of the pencil in my hand and drawing on some nice Bristol board. But I will admit I do miss the "undo" button. I like to see work penciled and inked on the same board. I do have a tablet PC that's about 3 years old now, and I try and do more color sketching on that. Coloring and painting is probably where I want to learn to use the computer better.

Veronese: What was it like to come back to comics with the *X-Men Legends/Ultimate Alliance series* and *X-Men Origins: Wolverine*? Any bit of nostalgia? One can make the argument that these games expose more people to comic books and their storylines than the actual periodicals themselves.

Moy: It was tremendously rewarding to work on those games. At Raven Software, there are a number of comic book fans that took it to heart to make the game experience really feel like the characters and world, because we knew if you miss a detail or don't present something right, the fans will hammer on you for it. Granted, it's a video game, so we do have to stretch some things. Dealing with the licensed games, I think it's still mostly people that know the characters that will buy that game, but yes, I think it does

Opposite: (top to bottom)
Star Trek Voyager: Elite Force game packaging

Jedi Knight II: Jedi Outcast screenshot and packaging

Above: (top to bottom)
X-Men: Legends packaging and concept art
X-Men Origins: Wolverine packaging

expose more people to the worlds that comics has to offer. Will it lead them into a comic store...maybe? Maybe not, but it could lead to more comic properties coming to games. *Scott Pilgrim,* I'm looking at you... yeah, baby!

Veronese: Have you ever worked on a game in a writing capacity?

Moy: Not in the formal sense. I'm much more down the line and collaborate more to solve issues, than to be the first idea guy. If something doesn't sound right or logical, I'll bring it up and at times there could be discussion on what can be done to make it work. But when you're working on a project with 40-100 people, everyone's got their own ideas and concerns, and it's up to the project leads to ultimately make those decisions. When I do storyboards for cinematics, I try and bring what I've learned from storytelling in comics to the boards and hope that it will transfer to the final edit; but again, it comes down to time and the decisions of the leads. I've brought up the idea about starting a writing team at Raven, to bounce ideas around and to streamline issues before they come up, but sadly that hasn't come to fruition, so I will continue to focus on concept work until it does.

Veronese: How did your side project, *Video Game Gals,* come about?

Moy: *Video Game Gals* is my creator-owned project. The first book is pretty much all penciled except for a couple of pages at the end. Its origin comes from an ashcan that several other artists and I contributed to based on the simple premise of girl fighting games. Probably one specifically called *Variable Geo,* strictly sold in Japan. After their appearance there, and between me looking for work after *Legionnaires,* I started to develop it into a property. By mashing elements from *Tron, Reboot, Quantum Leap,* and *Sliders,* I laid out the groundwork for the world of *Video Game Gals.* The story will start off

simply enough as this team of women that enter dimensional rifts to rescue hapless victims trapped in there and will expand in story and scope from there. The pages are about 10 years old now, but I think they still hold up, so one of these fine days, *Video Game Gals* will come to life in a European-style graphic novel. So stay tuned!

Veronese: Do you have any desire to move back into the comic industry full-time in the near future?

Moy: For now, I think Raven Software will be where I'm at. I take my career a bit more day-to-day and don't really think about it too much. I do continue to work on commissions for people at conventions and online and have just completed the second issue of *Lady Robotika* for Image Comics. My brother had to help me out as I think trying to get a monthly book done was way more than I could handle in addition to working a full-time job. I don't mind dipping my toes into comics, but I would need to find a project that allows me a bit more time to complete. If for whatever reason I'm not at Raven Software, I wouldn't mind seeing what comics could offer me in terms of work and stability, but I'll probably be exploring all my options in video games and storyboarding as well.

Veronese: Have you done any storyboarding work?

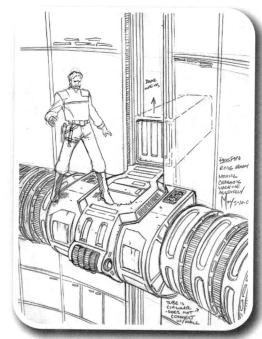

Moy: The only storyboarding that I have done was for the games I worked on. On *Star Wars Jedi Knight II: Jedi Outcast* we were pretty limited in the technology and concerns about close-ups and moving the camera around. Camera work was all programmed and animations were strung in there with it. There were some hilarious glitches during that time.

Veronese: What specific type of work did you do on *Star Wars*

Above:
Video Game Gals comic book

Left and Opposite:
Star Wars Jedi Knight II: Jedi Outcast concept art

Jedi Knight II: Jedi Outcast? Was there a learning curve involved in the transition from comics to video games?

Moy: Specifically, I was doing concepts for various environments and trying to learn the business and procedures on how games get made. The work was fairly easy, because they just asked me to draw when I first got there. After a couple months I started to help out by painting textures for objects. That was where I had to play catch-up and learn more about the technical side of creating art assets for games. Tasks like viewing models, working on a base page for the skin that goes on to the object, applying that to the object and seeing how it looks in the game were all things I had to learn since I had zero game experience and little computer knowledge.

Veronese: What is a typical day at Raven Software like for you?

Moy: A typical day for me is much like many office jobs, I'm guessing. I like to get in early, usually by 7 a.m., get some coffee, check emails for news or tasks and then get to work on said tasks. Often during the day, tasks are completed or new ones get assigned, so there are some meetings sprinkled in or just a little running around to get more information or direction on a project. I then try to determine how many drawings I might need to get done to help

define an environment. Sometimes it is one, sometimes it is four or more.

Veronese: Do you normally work on a single game as a team until it is completed, moving to different stages of art over time, or do you move from video game project to project?

Moy: For the most part, I'm usually on one project from start to finish. Until most recently I was working on *X-Men Origins: Wolverine*, and when that game was completed, I was assigned to the *Singularity* team. Joining midstream and trying to get caught up and find out how the team works and find a place where I could be the most useful was an interesting experience. I must say I prefer to follow through on one project from the beginning, since you can "see" the vision of

how the game looks and feels. At times like that, the best thing you can do is just maintain a professional attitude while getting acclimated to the new team.

Veronese: Do your work days change depending on the stage of completion of the game?

Moy: Over the course of a project there are times when were told to come in for a couple more hours per day or the weekend. The dreaded "crunch mode." This time usually comes at the end of a project when all the final aspects are polished, all the bugs are being worked out, and we're really driving to deliver a solid product that we can all be proud of. Crunch mode has always been a point of contention in the game industry. In comics, you typically work twelve hours or more out of the day, but it didn't ever feel like work, at least not to me. Maybe it is because most comic artists work from home, but the work just becomes part of your lifestyle.

Veronese: You mentioned using a Cintiq tablet. Did you go through a trial and error process with several tablets before finding the right one? Artists seem to be picky (and loyal) when it comes to their tablets.

Moy: Not really. The Cintiq I use is at Raven. Raven buys Cintiqs for most of the artists and modelers to use, so I really didn't have an option between different models. I'm not really aware there are other competitors in the Cintiq category since it's a very unique product. Now drawing tablets that sit next to your keyboard are ones I could not really get used to for drawing. There's too much of a departure in my brain to follow the cursor on the screen and what my hand is doing. For painting and textures, it was fine, but before the Cintiq, I would always do my concept work on paper. I'm not fully convinced I need a tablet at home yet.

Veronese: Are you a *Scott Pilgrim* fan? The 16-bit retro game based on the comic is a lot of fun. I think the movie could bring a lot of people into comics.

Moy: I'm a recent fan. When I started seeing the trailers for the movie, I thought it looked kind of cool and familiar, and then a coworker lent me the first five volumes of the trades and I breezed through them. I wasn't really into it until Volume Five and the way that one ended; I really enjoyed the story and characters. But I think it's awesome how the look and feel of the comic was able to be adapted to the movie and game. That's how I'd like to see more comic book properties handled, but it's a fine line. I'm also looking forward to the game. Actually as a developer, we have access to some games on XBox Live before their official release and can download and play them. I've done that with *Scott Pilgrim* but haven't had a chance to play it yet. It's another perk for being in this industry.

Veronese: Do you currently play video games in your spare time or does your work kill your love for the pastime?

Moy: I played tons of games as a wee lad. Our family had a lot of the early consoles: the Fairchild Channel F, an Odyssey II, the Atari 2600, an Intellivision, a ColecoVision, and the Vectrex. There were also the arcades that popped up, and lots of after school time was spent there. I kind of got out of games in high school and college and that lasted a bit even after college. Most of my free time was dedicated to drawing and comics. My brother would play various games on his PC, but I'd just watch for the most part when I wasn't drawing. It wasn't until I started working at Raven that I started playing games again. This time it was first-person shooters and *Counter Strike*, *Battlefield 1942*, and Raven Software's *Soldier of Fortune II*. For a while I was a PC shooter guy, but they started getting a bit too complex for me, so I stopped playing those and picked up *City of Heroes*, which still takes up my lunch hour.

For the most part, I'm a very casual gamer and my game of choice for that is *Rock Band*. I have fun playing it by myself and with other people that come over for a *Rock Band* night. I think *Galaga* and *Donkey Kong* still hold a special place in my heart. I'm so old school.

Veronese: I think I've seen your sketchbooks at a comic convention before. They are another outlet for the *Video Game Gals*, right?

Moy: Yep, currently the sketchbook is the only outlet to see the *Video Game Gals*. There are designs for them and various pinups I do of them as well as some Christmas card stuff I use them in. So if you see me at a con, please feel free to buy them until the graphic novel comes out.

Veronese: What's some of your favorite commission work to do?

Moy: I like to draw people of the more female persuasion. I will usually do just about anything. Superheroines are a staple of my commissions, particularly the lasses of the Legion of Superheroes. They're really still fun for me to draw and I still get plenty of requests for them online and at cons.

Veronese: Raven Software recently released the Cold War-themed first-person shooter *Singularity*, a game that really would translate well into a comic book (it's almost as if the story was based on a comic book that didn't exist). Could you tell us a little about the game? Were you involved in it's creation, and if so, what steps did you work on?

Moy: It's funny you should mention a comic book for it, because there's an incentive graphic novel that Amazon has when you purchase the game. I'm not sure how the story came about, but it tells a story about how the found the island of Katorga-12, an island that houses the rare element E-99. I don't think any of the developers were really aware of the comic until a preview was given out at 2009's San Diego Comic Con International. It would've been nice to work on the comic, but I think the deal was worked out at Activision through the corporate headquarters.

As for the game, it's about a special ops member (the player's character) that was on assignment to check out some anomalous reading coming from the island Katorga-12. A series of events happen, and the player becomes stranded on the abandoned island. While looking around, the players get sent back in time and finds out that he has altered history when he returns. At that point, it's up to you to solve the mystery of what happened on the island in the past and present and somehow set the timeline back in order. Oh, and there's a bunch of soldiers and mutated inhabitants out to kill you as well, but to combat them you have several awesome futuristic weapons at your disposal.

I wasn't on *Singularity* for the first few years of its development, but was assigned to it later on and helped finish the game. I started out doing storyboards for the cinematics and then I worked on the project by providing concept art when new directions or areas came up. They already had several concept artists working on the game when I went over, so it was just a matter of following their lead. Towards the end of the game I started play testing it to find bugs or just trying to "break" the game, or look for progression stoppers.

*[**Author's note:** The remainder is a follow-up interview performed after Jeffrey Moy returned to the comic book industry.]*

Veronese: Why did you leave the video game field? What was the last project you worked on?

Moy: It wasn't by choice. Raven made the decision to concentrate on one project instead of three, and with that comes redundancy, so people were unfortunately let go. There was one layoff at Raven Software in the year before I was let go, so there were those who saw the writing on the wall. I wasn't one of them. I continued to work in a professional manner and do my job to the best of my abilities, but these things happen. I'm not bitter or angry about it. I don't think anyone really can work one job as a career these days until they reach the age of retirement. I'm glad to have worked at Raven with great people and on some really great projects. *Singularity* was the last game I worked on that was published while I was there. I did work on some of the downloadable content map packs for *Call of Duty: Black Ops*, so you'll see my name in the credits.

Veronese: You've come full circle now. What has it been like coming back to comics?

Moy: I have to say it was a lot of fun coming back and having a story published. *Lady Robotika* was a bit rushed, but being able to work with the Legion characters, as well as ones you help create is always fun. How could it not be?

Veronese: Was there a story to go along with your return to comics? Has it been an unusual transition back, especially with the lack of structure in the comic book production process at times?

Moy: Not really. It's pretty typical for freelance artists to put feelers out there, get in touch with contacts, and the *Adventure Comics* project came about through my brother, Phil, sending an email to Brian Cunningham, an editor at DC looking for work and throwing my name in there. A couple weeks later and we received an email asking us if we would like to do an XS (a speedster member of the Legionnaires) back-up story that Paul Levitz wrote with us in mind. Story continuity was something I had not done in a while, but after working on *Lady Robotika*, I was feeling it come back to me. Doing roughs, layouts, backgrounds…it's like riding a bike, but I wanted to try to add more to what I've done before, otherwise it doesn't feel like you've grown as an artist. For the most part, I don't really feel like I have grown in terms of my comic work. I would like to incorporate more of a manga-esque storytelling in to my comic book art, but the manga influence will have to come through osmosis as I really don't like to force myself to do it. There's something to be said about drawing page after page, month after month, that really makes you improve or lose your mind. I find myself getting used to the routine I had when I was working in comics ten years ago and that seemed to work out well.

Veronese: What are some of your upcoming comic book projects?

Moy: Currently I have projects with publishers, but I'm hoping to land something that I just received word of that sounds up my alley. Granted, even if I do get it, it's only for a finite time and comic work can be feast or famine. We'll have to see if I'm able to continue to get steady work in comics. If I can, then I could be around for a while. If not, I have to be realistic once again and look elsewhere for opportunities where someone can use my talents on a regular paying basis.

Opposite:
Singularity game packaging

Above:
Singularity screenshot

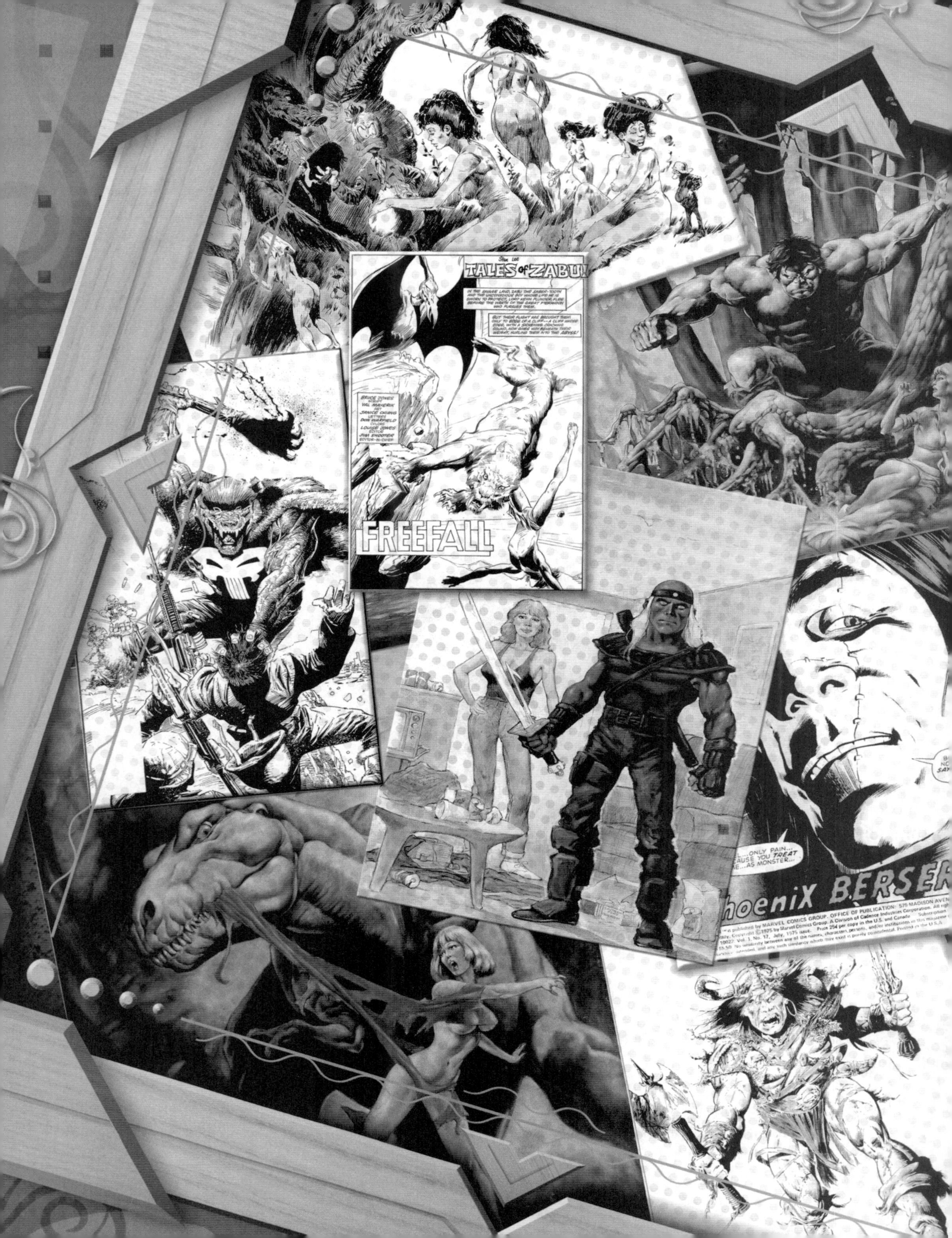

TALES of ZABU!
BRUCE JONES SCRIPT
VAL MAYERIK ART
JANICE CHIANG LETTERS
DON WARFIELD COLORS
LOUISE JONES EDITOR
JIM SHOOTER EDITOR-IN-CHIEF
FREEFALL
...ONLY PAIN...
...AS MONSTER...
BERSER
MARVEL COMICS GROUP. OFFICE OF PUBLICATION: 575 MADISON AVEN
Copyright ©1975 by Marvel Comics Group. A Division of Cadence Industries Corporation.
Vol. 1, No. 17, July, 1975 issue.

Val**Mayerik**

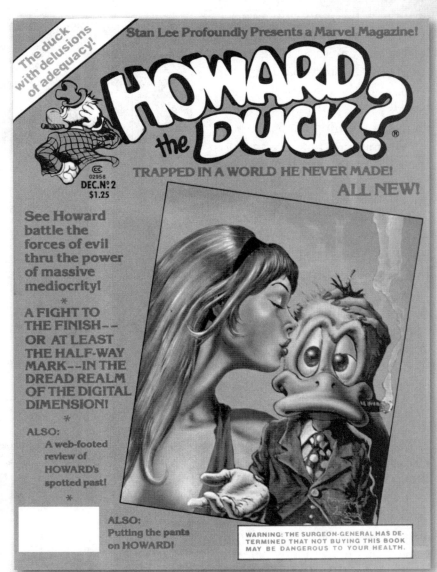

Best known for his role in creating Howard the Duck, Val Mayerik broke into the comic book industry with Marvel Comics, penciling horror stories and barbarian tales in the early 1970s. A stint on *Adventure into Fear*, a title featuring Man-Thing, led Mayerik and writer Steve Gerber to introduce Howard the Duck to the Marvel Universe. Mayerik would go on to illustrate the *Howard the Duck* syndicated comic strip in the following years. Mayerik currently works in the field of commercial illustration, designing storyboards and concept art for video games and television commercials for Microsoft and Coca-Cola.

Veronese: What work did you do for the *Grand Theft Auto* series?

Mayerik: My work in video games is not too expansive; I did some comp work a few years back for *Grand Theft Auto*. I work for an ad agency that does ad spots for Electronic Arts and so I have storyboarded the commercial spots for their games. All in all the work experience has been satisfactory and uneventful.

Veronese: How would you describe the difference between a "comp" and a storyboard? Do you approach them differently?

Opposite: (left to right)
Howard the Duck illustration, *The Hulk Magazine* #10, *The Punisher* #78, *Ka-Zar The Savage* #2 interior page, Marvel Graphic Novel #11: *Void Indigo*, *Frankenstein* #17 interior page, *Eerie* #97 cover art and *Conan* Annual #8

Above:
Howard the Duck Magazine #2

Mayerik: A comp is a drawing or illustration that is simply meant to be a visual guide or representation for what will become a print ad in a magazine, packaging imagery, or any imagery used for promotion. Storyboards are sequential graphic narratives, similar to comics, that are used to show how a commercial spot, TV or viral, will be shot and give a rough idea what the spot may look like. Sometimes spots end up following the storyboarding and sometimes the director uses the boards as a departure point and creates something different.

Veronese: What are some of the advertising campaigns you have worked on for Electronic Arts?

Mayerik: I have worked on a variety of ad pitches for Electronic Arts. One was their WWII game, I believe it was *Call of Duty 3*. Also, I have done work for some of the *Sims* games, but I don't remember which ones specifically. Another larger project was *Dante's Inferno*. On all of these projects I simply storyboarded ad ideas that were then presented to EA for approval. And too, as is always the case some of this line of work, some of the ad ideas made it to production and some did not. I also did some character design for *Dante's Inferno*, which was a nice change.

Veronese: Are there any similarities between storyboard work and comics? Do you prefer one over the other?

Mayerik: Storyboarding and comics in theory are similar in that they are telling stories with pictures. The frame size is uniform in storyboarding and in comics, of

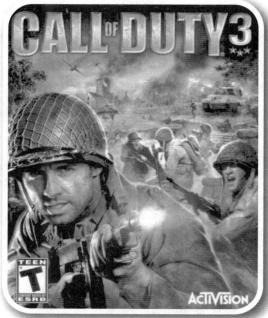

course, the panel size and shape can vary greatly. I like doing storyboards; comics work these days is sporadic and the business is now very much different than when I was highly active in it, so it is difficult to compare the two fairly. I feel comfortable now doing storyboards and believe that it has probably improved my comic book skills as much as it has made my storytelling more concise.

Veronese: Is there a comic project you worked on in the past that you feel would translate well into a video game?

Mayerik: I did a series with Larry Hama back in the 1980s about a young samurai titled the *Young Master*. I think it would make a great video game.

Veronese: What is your typical work day like? How does it differ than working in comics?

Mayerik: It differs a great deal—advertising deadlines are much more time sensitive. When working in the comic book industry, deadlines could be as long as two to three months down the line. Advertising deadlines are usually due for same day or the next day, with an extention sometimes to two days, but that is rare.

Veronese: How long have you been working on the web comic *Useful Idiots*? The Internet is a great distribution channel for comics. How did *Useful*

***Above:** (top to bottom)*
Grand Theft Auto packaging

Call of Duty 3 figures

Call of Duty 3 packaging art

Idiots come about? I like the reference in the title to Cold War sympathizers—was it intentional?

Mayerik: I was asked to do *Useful Idiots* by James Hudnall, the writer on *Useful Idiots*. We met about two and a half years ago and hit it off right away, not just on politics but we both like the same kind of comics, films, art etc. Also, yes, the *Useful Idiots* reference is indeed the one you mention though I think it predates the Cold War and is attributed to Trotsky or Lenin.

Veronese: With a turnaround that short on storyboard and advertisement work (1-2 days), what kind of reference information and direction are you given?

Mayerik: I work from a script that is put together by a creative director and a copy writer. They provide any reference that is needed; this could be anything from a celebrity athlete or a pictorial reference of past campaigns. I have found most creative people in advertising delightfully easy to work with, which in my experience, was not always the case in comics.

Veronese: Did you particularly enjoy working on any of the Electronic Arts games? The *Dante's Inferno* art looks great. The game was accompanied by an extremely well-executed ad campaign.

Mayerik: I have indeed enjoyed working on EA pitches. It is a genre game that provides a departure from the conventional ad campaigns, although I like working on those as well. Working *Dante's Inferno* was fun,

USEFUL IDIOTS

By James Hudnall and Val Mayerik

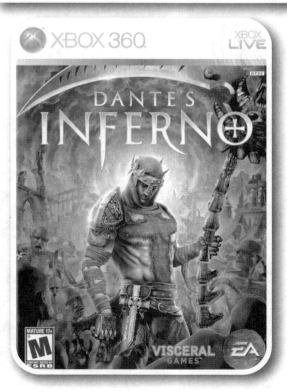

but I particularly enjoyed the WWII stuff I did with EA as I've always wanted to do a WWII comic.

Veronese: Do you play video games or have you played them in the past? If so, are you a console or PC game? Do you have any favorite games?

Mayerik: I do NOT play video games and probably never will. I have no axe to grind against video games; it just never caught on with me. Part of the reason, I am sure, is generational. The video game phenomenon came into its own when I was already in my late thirties and shortly there after I purchased my first Mac. Also, I was never a gaming fan of any kind. I have done a lot of work for Wizards of the Coast over the years but have never once played *Magic: The Gathering*. I think it is a particular kind of mentality that is attracted to that type of activity. That is not to say that I don't like the genres represented in these games; I just prefer to read or view films. My son is in his early twenties and in a pre-med program and hardly plays video games at all. I train in martial arts and ride horses; I'm much more real-world oriented. However, I am aware that it is a multi-billion dollar industry and am glad to lend a helping hand where I can.

Above: (top to bottom)
Useful Idiots #1 web comic

Dante's Inferno packaging

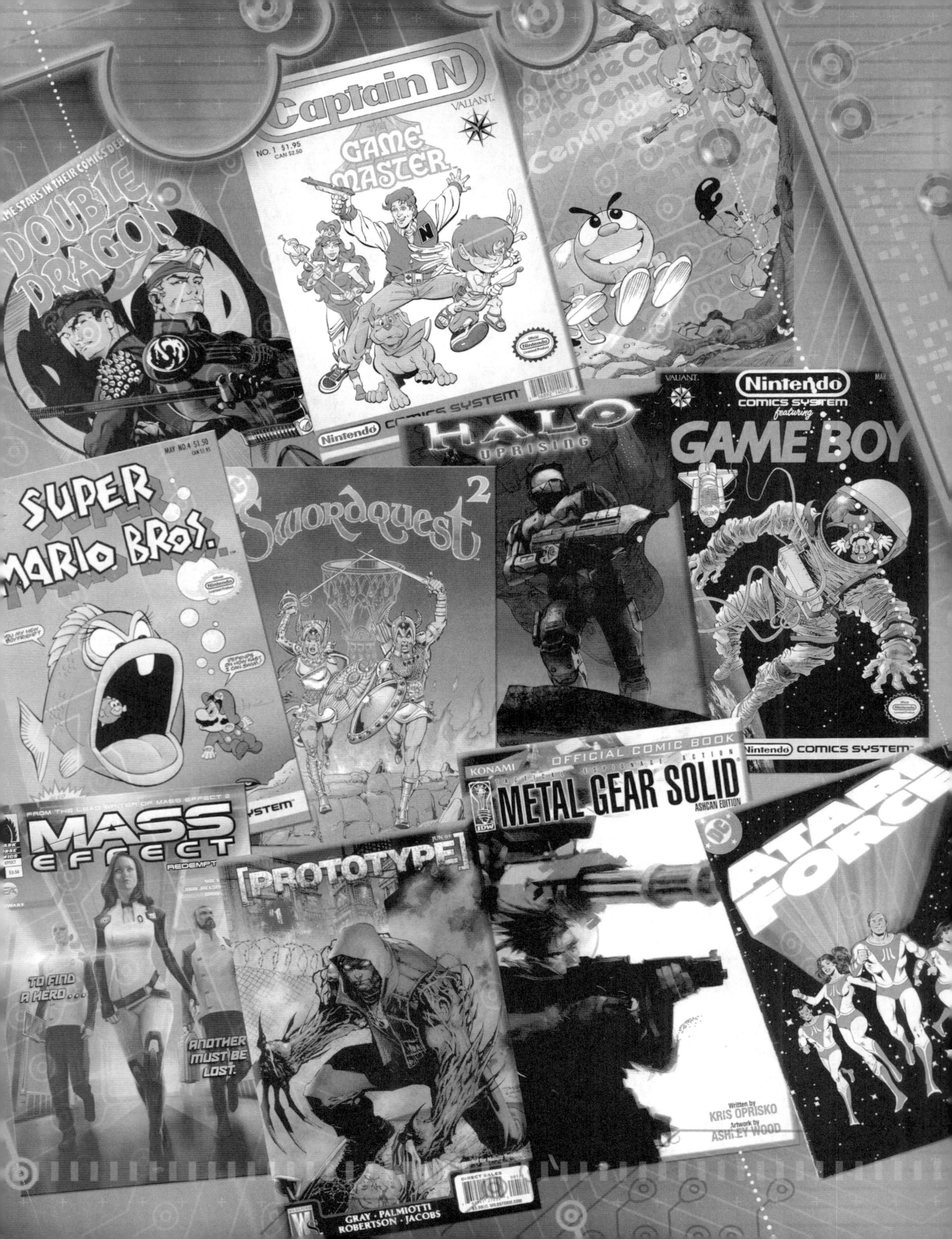

Captain N
VALIANT
NO. 1 $1.95
CAN $2.50
GAME MASTER
Nintendo COMICS SYSTEM
DOUBLE DRAGON
Centipede
Nintendo
COMICS SYSTEM
featuring
GAME BOY
HALO
UPRISING
MAY NO.4 $1.50
SUPER MARIO BROS.
Swordquest 2
OFFICIAL COMIC BOOK
KONAMI
METAL GEAR SOLID
ASHCAN EDITION
FROM THE LEAD WRITER OF MASS EFFECT 2
MASS EFFECT
TO FIND A HERO...
ANOTHER MUST BE LOST.
[PROTOTYPE]
GRAY · PALMIOTTI
ROBERTSON · JACOBS
Written by
KRIS OPRISKO
Artwork by
ASHLEY WOOD
ATARI FORCE

POWER-**UP:**
Video Games Invade
Comic Books

Look at the back of any comic book from the 1980s—I bet it is emblazoned with a wacky, over-the-top advertisement for a video game. Thanks to the overlap of audience demographics, using comic books to spread the word about newly released console games was a no-brainer, with ads for video games filling not only the back covers of Marvel and DC Comics well into the 1990s and the present. While many video game franchises made an aggressive foray into the comic book market by producing comics based on their franchises, most were met with mixed results.

Marvel Produces An Early Video Game Magazine

Marvel produced seven issues of the comic book-sized magazine *Blip* beginning in 1983, one of the first attempts to tie-in video games with the world of comic books. *Blip* was also one of the first periodicals dedicated solely to video games, mixing interviews with teenage celebrities, previews of upcoming games, top scores reported by mail, and tips and tricks to capitalize on the early 1980s arcade craze. While *Blip* did not last very long, it helped set the stage for the video game periodicals *Electronic Gaming Monthly* and *GamePro*. *Blip* #1 is of particular interest to back issue collectors, as it features the first comic book appearance of Donkey Kong and the Super Mario Brothers.

DC used its editorial and writing talent to help out fellow Time Warner commodity Atari by creating the *Atari Force* in 1982. The characters of A.T.A.R.I. Force (Advanced Technology And Research Institute) did not directly tie-in to any existing video games. The team scoured the universe looking for a new home for the human race, all while wearing stylish costumes emblazoned with the Atari logo. The first *Atari Force* series was

Opposite:
Double Dragon #1, Captain N #1, Centipede #1, Super Mario Bros. #4, Swordquest #2, Halo Uprising #1, Game Boy #2, Mass Effect #4, Prototype #1, Metal Gear Solid Ashcan Edition, and *Atari Force #1*

Top:
Mega Man #1

Above:
Blip Magazine #1

created as a line of mini-comics to be packed in with popular Atari games like *Defender* and *Berzerk*. DC was also putting top art talent on the series in the form of Dick Giordano and Gil Kane. After the series of promotional mini-comics, DC published a twenty-issue *Atari Force* series written by Gerry Conway, which concentrated on science-fiction aspects rather than promotional elements, and featured art by José Luis García-López and Ross Andru. Atari also created a sword-and-sorcery comic book, *Swordquest*, in tandem with DC and Roy Thomas. Using secrets revealed within the *Swordquest* video game and comic book, players could win a diamond-studded, 18-karat gold talisman and additional medieval prizes.

Taking Care of a Franchise

Valiant Comics, in their first incarnation, supported itself solely on entities licensed from Nintendo, creating the Nintendo Comics System imprint in 1990. Choosing to tie-in with Nintendo allowed the company to reach a wide variety of customers, with the comics selling on the shelves of Toys 'R Us and other unconventional comic retailers in addition to comic book shops. Valiant regularly published the *Adventures of the Super Mario Brothers*, a comic featuring the walking Nintendo billboard *Captain N*; *Legend of Zelda*; and a number of specials before moving on to the superhero genre. Valiant Comics added to the Nintendo mythos by creating Dirk Drain-Head, a comic book superhero whom Mario idolizes.

Archie Comics took a leap of faith by licensing Sega's *Sonic the Hedgehog*, beginning with a four-issue limited series that turned into a 250+ issue series that is still going strong. *Sonic the Hedgehog* is the longest ongoing series to feature a video game character. The series routinely outsells many Marvel and DC titles while providing an opportunity to bring kids and video game fans into retail comic book stores. Archie

culled comic book talent to create a book in the style of the video game, with writer Mark Millar and long-time Marvel inker Terry Austin working with the character. Millar did his work on Sonic as a part of Fleetway UK's *Sonic the Comic* series, where he also wrote stories based on Sega's *Streets of Rage* video game.

Archie's *Sonic* franchise has spurred a number of spinoffs, and led the publisher to pursue the rights of other video game commodities like Capcom's *Mega Man*. Archie's work in keeping the flagship character of Japanese video game giant Sega in the limelight every month did a wellspring of good for Sega Corporation, ensuring the company's brand significance after the failure of the Sega Dreamcast and their subsequent exit from video game console manufacturing.

While Valiant and Archie sought to establish long-term ties with licenses, DC and Marvel looked to shorter term mini-series. One of the more forgettable series was Marvel's six-issue *Double Dragon* mini-series. While the video game was one of the hits of the 1980s and 1990s, succeeding in both console and arcade form, the comic book fizzled thanks to a lack of a direct connection to the game, as the costumes and characters were altered to make for a better comic fit. One bright spot of the series was its covers, which featured art by Tom Raney, Larry Stroman, Kevin Maguire, Steve Lightle, and Arthur Adams.

Independent publishers created multiples iterations of titles based on the popular video game series *Street Fighter*, *Resident Evil*, *Tomb Raider*, and *World of WarCraft*, but with little success. These comics were often created first as a promotional tool, and second as a quality comic, with the video games themselves often lacking little story to tell other than a regurgitation of the video game's plot. This is one place Archie and the *Sonic the Hedgehog* franchise succeeded—the writers and artists fleshed out a whole universe and continue to do so with the series, so much so that the out of continuity series

Sonic X, was created to tell stories not fitting within the confines of the Sonic-verse.

A Move to Quality

The *Metal Gear Solid* series is another great example of a successful fusion between comic books and video games. The IDW-published series did not stray far from the storyline of the video games, a storyline often regarded as one of the best in the history of video games. The series made an interesting art choice, going with the unconventional Ashley Wood instead of aiming for an artist with a photo-realistic style. The decision to pick Wood led to much of the success of the series, with Wood's art now synonymous with Konami's flagship series. Wood also created art for use in the video game *Metal Gear Solid: Peacewalker*, further tying the video game and comic book worlds together.

Marvel Comics tapped Brian Michael Bendis to write the first of many *Halo* mini-series. 2007's *Halo: Uprising* tells the story of the invasion of Cleveland, Ohio, Bendis' hometown, by Covenant invaders. Instead of focusing on *Halo* star Master Chief, the *Halo: Uprising* gives the perspective of local residents and everyday individuals struggling against the invasion. Marvel continues to put top-level comic book talent, including Peter David, on series taking place in the world of *Halo*, creating an impressive product that sells well and furthers the *Halo* backstory.

Epic Games chose the DC imprint Wildstorm to publish an ongoing series based on the *Gears of War* franchise, hiring comic book and video game veteran Joshua Ortega to write the series while picking Simon Bisley and Liam Sharp to re-create the gritty visuals of the *Gears* universe. The series is one of the best video game tie-in comics to date, as it set the stage and introduced characters that appeared in later installments of the *Gears of War* video game franchise while covering stories that would be impossible to tell in a video game.

Jim Lee confirmed that *Gears of War #1* was the best-selling comic book of 2008, outselling DC's own mega-crossover *Final Crisis* and the return of Barry Allen to the land of the living in the DC Universe. Part of these additional sales came through the unconventional venues available for selling video game tie-in comic books like rental stores, video game stores, and mass market retailers.

Thanks to the success of the *Gears of War, Metal Gear Solid*, and *Halo* series, almost every major video game release receives an accompanying comic book title, for better or worse. Some video game companies release a comic book tie-in to create publicity in the months prior to release, with this technique working well for *Prototype, Diablo III, Infamous*, and the *Assassin's Creed* franchise. The focus in these situations is not necessarily on content, but gaining an additional avenue of exposure.

While some modern video game comics serve merely as promotional tools, Dark Horse's *Mass Effect* series became a viable comic book title by expanding on the stories told in the mega-hit science-fiction role-playing game. Dark Horse has experienced an enormous amount of success and continues to bring people into comic book stories with their series of *Mass Effect* spin-offs. These comics do not simply re-tell the stories from the video game in a condensed form, but like novels, yield a plethora of new information about main and auxiliary characters, giving fans a chance to visit their favorite universes long after the video game adventures are over.

Enjoy the following chats with Roy Thomas, Gerry Conway, and Elliot S! Maggin about the very early days of integrating comic books and video games, and time they spent working with Atari. We will also talk with writer Joshua Ortega about his work about their work creating the story for *Gears of War 2* and *Gears of War 3* as well as the DC/Wildstorm spin-off comic book.

Opposite:
Sonic The Hedgehog #239

Above:
Gears of War #1

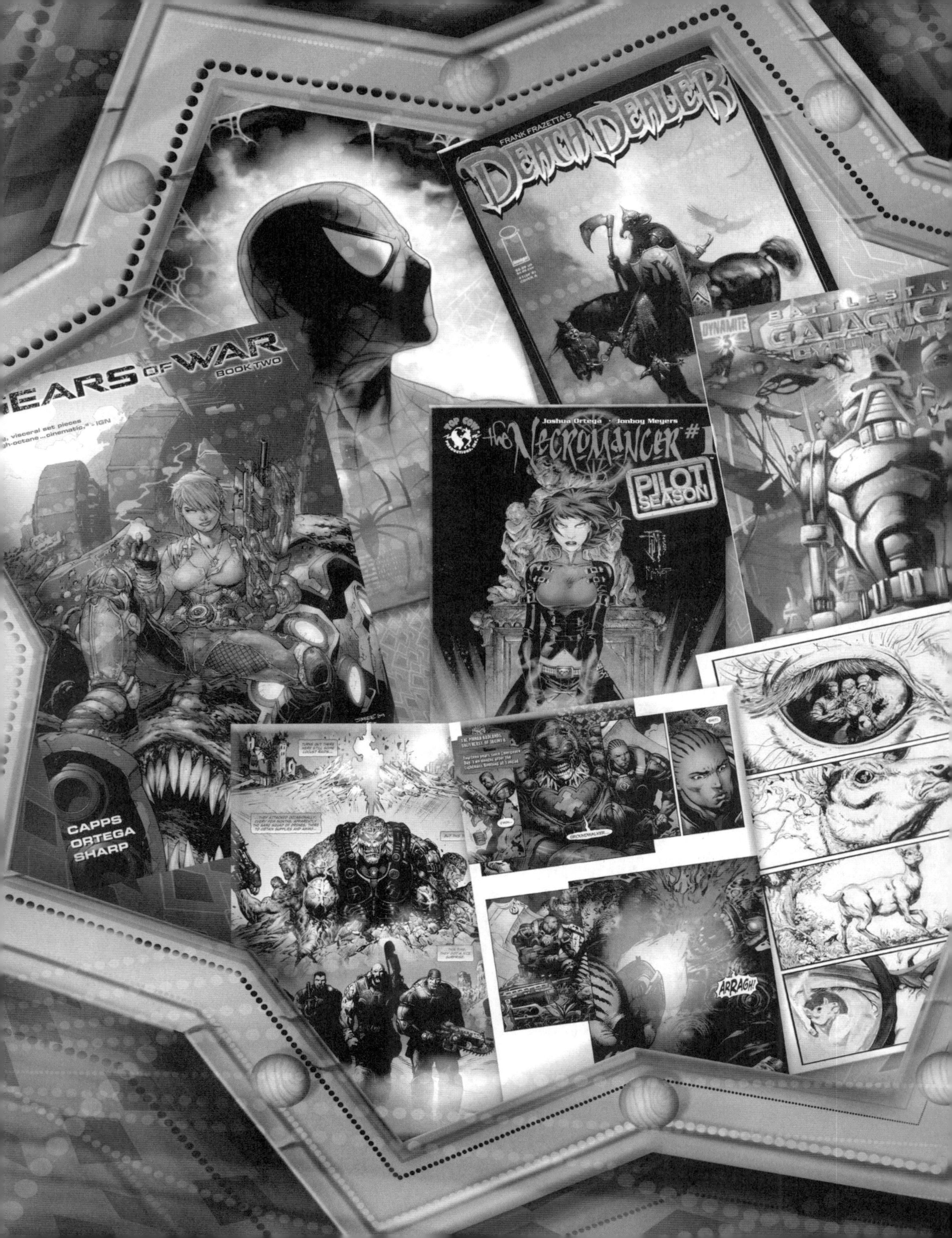
FRANK FRAZETTA'S
DEATH DEALER
DYNAMITE
GALACTICA
EARS OF WAR
BOOK TWO
Joshua Ortega · Jonboy Meyers
the NECROMANCER #
PILOT SEASON
CAPPS
ORTEGA
SHARP
GROUNDWALKER...
ARRAGH!

Joshua**Ortega**

Critically acclaimed author of the novel ((Frequencies)), Joshua Ortega's extensive experience weaves through a number of creative fields. Ortega has penned comic book scripts for *Battlestar Galactica*, *The Necromancer*, *Red Sonja*, *Spider-Man Unlimited*, and Frank Frazetta's *Death Dealer*. Ortega also worked on Epic Games' *Gears of War 2* and *3* along with a plethora of projects produced by Microsoft Studios. He is currently working on a sequel to his novel ((Frequencies)), entitled ~Vibrations~, with Joshua aiming to take advantage of bleeding edge technology available in the e-book realm to create a reader experience like none other.

Keith Veronese: What were your writing duties for *Gears of War 2*? Was the game scaffolding already in place when you joined the team?

Joshua Ortega: For *Gears 2*, the game already had a lot of scaffolding in place—Cliff Bleszinski and the production team already had a lot of the game in place. I came in a lot later than what was really ideal, but it was just how things lined up. I was freed up on another project, and Epic Games really was ready for a writer to step in. Susan O'Connor wrote the first *Gears of War*, and did a great job, but there were a lot of other projects going on and I think everybody was looking for something new direction-wise, so it was a really amicable parting. I was freed up from another project at Xbox just in time, and Cliff Bleszinski and I were already friends. He asked me to send over some samples as soon as I could. Epic really liked the samples, and they brought me on quickly after that. Then there was a real "crunch time" to write the first draft of the script, I had to get it out in a couple of months and it was a lot of pages. The scaffolding of the game was there, but I still got in at an early enough stage where I could bring a lot to the story. For example, the Maria scene—that was a big scene for me that I wanted to bring into the game. That and Tai's suicide scene—I seem to have brought in all the really brutal parts of *Gears of War 2*.

I was still able to affect the story a lot. There was no Chairman Prescott in the initial version. In the script before, we needed a leader, and another character was being used as a placeholder to give the big speech in the third act. I wanted a presidential type figure—something that would flesh

Opposite: (left to right)
Spider-Man Unlimited #8, Death Dealer #1, Gears of War: Book 2, The Necromancer #1: Pilot Season, Battlestar Galactica: Cylon War #3, Gears of War #3 interior page, *Gears of War #1* interior page and *The Other Dead #1* interior page

Above:
((Frequencies))

this world out. A lot of these things got cut from the first *Gears of War* game because of the tight ship date—it is a great story, but it also left us a lot of room to maneuver with in *Gears of War 2*. We were really able to expand the world and the mythology around *Gears*, so it was a great time to come onto the franchise. A lot of scaffolding was in place, but there was also a lot of possibilities where we could move the scaffolding, interject a lot of story elements, and work with the team tightly. Things definitely changed—that was one of the things that Cliff (Bleszinski) always told me about video games as I was coming into the industry. He told me to, "Get ready, you're just going to have to write for the technology sometimes." Unlike with a comic or a movie, you can't re-shoot something, re-cast a character, re-draw a character, or sometimes we just can't model a character, and that would mean that character just disappears from the story, and whatever reverberates from there, you will just have to write for that. That was great advice.

Veronese: Cliff seems like a genius—especially after interacting with several people who have worked with him.

Ortega: He is a genius. I 100% agree. He got a lot of sh*t there for using the "Cliffy B" moniker and being the celebrity face of video games for a lot of years. That's part of the reason he dropped the name Cliffy B; he just thought he was giving people to much fuel. I thought it was fun; it was hip hop, I love it. I come from a hip hop music and journalism background, and it was a video game hip hop name, something like Jay-Z. It works, I understood what he was trying to do.

Veronese: The "Cliffy B" name worked at the time; it was MTV, it was the late 1990s.

Ortega: It was a very important time in video game history and we needed someone to step up and bear the burden of seeing that this was something cool. Cliff wants people to look at him and want to be like him, see that he's doing intelligent work, and that he's having fun living life too, living a dream making games and driving a Lamborghini to work.

Kids want to do this now, and I think he's influenced that. One of the number one jobs kids want to do is work in video games.

Veronese: And you have to be smart to do it.

Ortega: And that's one of the things people were trying to take away from him for a while. Cliff's been coding since he was 17. He's in his mid-thirties, but he's twenty years deep in the industry.

Veronese: He's one of those people who could succeed at whatever he wanted to do; he's got that sort of intelligence and drive.

Ortega: I don't toss the term genius around lightly, but with Cliff, it fits. He's taught me so much about the video game industry, and he just has an uncanny knack for what he calls "stickiness"—what makes people want to come in and play a game. I've seen him walk in and assess a play test and in ten minutes tell them to change this, this, and work on this, and it all works. He returns the compliments as well, and I've been able to show him a lot of writing techniques, since I can usually assess a story very well and quickly. It's fun, we're a good team.

Veronese: Do you have any ties to *Gears of War 3*?

Ortega: For *Gears of War 3* I came on as the initial story consultant. Cliff and I were the first two people to design number three, and it went down the ladder from there. That was a great experience to work with Cliff in that manner, and we handed it off after we completed the entire story. It was almost the opposite of the work I did for *Gears of War 2*, where I started with the game scaffolding; this time we designed the scaffolding. I turned over the scripting duties to Karen Traviss (author of the *City of Pearl* series, along with a series of *Star Wars* novels and the *Gears of War* novel series). I just had other stuff I wanted to do at the time, but it was a really fun trip. It was kind of like there were almost two different methods of working between the second and third *Gears of*

Above:
Gears of War #2 packaging art

Opposite:
Gears of War screen grab

War games, and I got to do both of them, working from the scaffolding in the second and creating the scaffolding for the third.

Veronese: That's very interesting, especially with Jace playing a role in *Gears of War 3*. When did the idea of *Gears of War* tie-in comic series come into play during the production of *Gears of War 2*?

Ortega: Epic knew they wanted to do a comic book series, and part of the reason they were excited when I came on for *Gears of War 2* was due to my background in comics. Mike Capps (President of Epic Games) and I talked about how we wanted to approach the comic. We were talking about bring in another writer for the comic since I was so busy with the scripting duties for the game, but I knew I could nail it and do what we wanted to do and do it right. It was a little more work, but I was so immersed in the universe at the time, I just thought it would make for a more cohesive experience for the franchise. The *Gears of War* franchise is just a golden egg of opportunities—it's a super franchise, and needs to be taken care of. Epic sees the potential as well, and believes in it, and that's why we worked so well together. This is just the beginning—the *Gears of War* franchise will be far bigger in five years than it is now, and that's saying a lot. Especially by the time the *Gears of War 3* marketing campaign rolls out, it will be on the tip on non-gamers' tongues just like the *Grand Theft Auto, Call of Duty,* and *Halo* series are.

One of the things I love so much about *Gears*, and something that will help it grow as a franchise, is that it has humanity; it has faces, there are characters. We have such a great roster of characters, something a lot of other franchises are missing. Every once in a while I want to compare *Gears* to *Star Wars* due to the strength in the number and depth of characters. You could literally make 40 different action figures out of the characters in *Gears,* that's something few franchises, especially video game franchises, can do. *Star Wars, Transformers, G.I. Joe, He-Man,* they could do that, and *Gears* is one of those magic franchises.

Veronese: That even goes back to what you mentioned about the first *Gears of War* game setting up the story, kind of like *A New Hope* did, and now you get to expand it with *Gears of War 2* and *3*.

Ortega: Yeah, you got it. And with the tie-in with the comic book series, I was starting to write and create Jace Stratton with Liam Sharp (Jace's co-designer). Liam did a great job creating the visuals for Jace; I love how he put the cornrows in. I didn't want to give Liam too much direction, I told Liam he was going to be half white/half black. The main thing that I wanted to remind him is that the Gears are always in armor and the player is looking at the character from a third-person perspective, so the character has to have a unique head. Liam did a great job with doing that and using the cornrows to pull that off, it was perfect. Part of the reason I created Jace was in response to Coltrane. Coltrane got a lot of criticism in the first *Gears of War* game, and admittedly, in isolation, he is a bit of a stereotype. An athletic, loud, strong black male. So to balance it out, we made a black character that is more of an everyday guy, and the minute we make that character, we have a spectrum, and you can't criticize Coltrane anymore. It's a spectrum. If you have a female character with large breasts, make one with small breasts, and then there is nothing you can criticize. Some people are loud, some people are quiet. Removing the criticism of Coltrane was a very big aspect for me in the creation of Jace.

Veronese: Jace is a great character from the reader's prospective, as he is as close to the reader seems to get to identifying with one of the Gears.

Ortega: I agree, even more than Dom. Dom sort of serves that role the games up to this point, but he

is still a bit over the top. I really wanted Jace to be ultrahuman—the new guy. Dom was so hardcore, he's just a little too badass for the player or reader to identify with.

Veronese: And that's what Jace is—he's the guy who has seen the horrors of the orphanages and goes out of his way to do the right thing.

Ortega: Thanks. I meant it to be that way. While creating Jace, I was just starting to write the comics. We were finishing the final pickup session for *Gears of War 2*; we were patching things up and then the game would be done. Right as I was creating Jace for the comic, we were in the recording studio, and I wanted to do one line of Jace audio for the game. It's right as they are dropping into The Hollow, just to be

depth to the backstory in a minimal amount of time if done well, but not bog down the gameplay as the individual player decides whether or not to participate.

Ortega: I wrote all the collectibles in *Gears of War 2*. That was actually a lot of work, but a lot of fun too. Those kind of bits and pieces of information can have a huge impact, and really immerse the player in the story. The collectibles were a wonderful opportunity to make a transmedia experience and expand the story. I've never seen a project so inter-connected. We had such a tight, small team work on the game (Cliff, Mike, Ron, and myself). That's the only way we pulled it off and we kept it all from becoming fragmented. With the collectibles, I also saw a wonderful opportunity to construct a meta-

a quick hint before the comic came out. It worked great, and helped the comic to bridge both the first and second video games and the mythology itself. A lot of players caught the audio snippet, and immediately picked up on Jace as being a familiar character in *Gears of War #1*. That came off well, and I've always tried to find little things to weave in between the game and the comic. There are a lot of hints and callbacks in the first six issues of the series.

Veronese: Who writes the "collectible" information in the game (the artifacts the player can choose to look for, like monument descriptions and left behind letters)? This is one of my favorite parts of video games that use this feature, as they can add tremendous

narrative; not just have them be an assembly of random facts, but I wanted to tell a story, and that became Sgt. Jonathan Harper's story. He has five or six pieces through the game, telling how he got the "rust lung" and escapes from The Hollow, saves a girl, and dies at the end. I was able to tell his story as well in the comic, in *Gears of War #8*, "Harper's Story." I was able to bring the collectible meta-narrative into the comic itself, and the fans really liked the weaving in and out between the forms of media. Epic gave me a lot of freedom to do this, and they liked it.

Veronese: One of the cool things about the collectibles was the insight it gave to the Horde. I remember one of the bits of collectible information saying something along the lines of, "If humanity loses to a bunch of things that talk to worms, we deserve to become extinct."

Ortega: Yeah, and the Horde is something we've kept as sort of a mystery. That becomes a fun story to tell. It was like a game of baiting to see how much we should tell. The entire backstory is worked out, but it's kind of like Darth Vader—you don't want to find out about him right away. Let the player learn about them as they progress. You get some hints with the Outpost level in *Gears of War 2*, but we've been saving some hints.

Veronese: What was a typical work day like while writing *Gears of War 2*? Did you have much communication with the rest of the production team?

Ortega: I was immersed; I worked a hell of a lot of hours. Back-to-back one hundred hour weeks. Sometimes, I was co-directing in the office studio from 8:30 a.m. to 6:30 p.m., then writing the script at night and picking up PR, writing the comic, and other stuff for the game like the collectibles information along the way. We were doing a war game, and at times it felt like a war, but I kept coming back. I was very much in tight with the production team too, I was brought in to all the meetings with the art leads, audio, everything. Epic was and is wonderful to work with. They show a great level of respect for art and the artists. You don't always see that with some publishers, but most developers really seem to respect the art.

Veronese: Epic Games seems to really try to grasp hold of quality artists and writers from other fields and get really great work out of them.

Ortega: Epic is great. I've always wanted to work with them. I worked on *Shadow Complex* for them too.

Veronese: The Orson Scott Card Xbox Live game?

Ortega: Yeah—I was story consultant on *Shadow Complex* and did some re-writes on the script. Peter David did the original script.

Veronese: I wish that would not have been an Xbox Live Arcade downloadable exclusive game from one point of view. It was so good and evolved, but I don't think it got the recognition it deserved since you couldn't pick up a physical copy and buy it.

Ortega: That's kinda true. It was part of the early roll out of Xbox Live Arcade for the Xbox 360. Chair Entertainment and Donald Mustard did a great job with the game. I had a conversation with Donald at San Diego Comic Con last year—he's a great mind and teacher.

Veronese: What was it like co-writing with Epic Games President Michael Capp for the "Barren" storyline on the *Gears of War* comic? Was that a story both of you wanted to tell so you worked together on it?

Ortega: That's a really interesting story that shined a lot on the creative collaboration process for me. One of the first things I asked when I came onto *Gears of War 2* was if we could get women in the game. Where are all the female characters in the *Gears* Universe? That all played into Cliff's advice about writing to the available technology—there wasn't enough time or resources to model a female character within the necessary project timeline. I tried to push it a little more, but it didn't go through. I try to ask once, if it gets shot down ask another time, then if it doesn't clear a second, I don't usually push a third, I just drop it. They loved the idea, but the time to spend on the modeling just wasn't available.

When the *Gears of War* comic came around, I wanted us to introduce females in the comic. We wouldn't be bound by technological constraints and that could set us up for some story development in *Gears of War 3*. So we set it up in the comic and introduce our first female Gear, Alex, who was co-designed by Jim Lee, and then bring in Sam for *Gears of War 3*.

To pull this off though, we needed to come up with a logical explanation as to why there were not female Gears in the first *Gears of War* game, as part of the comic takes place between the first game and its sequel. I was inspired by Margaret Atwood's *The Handmaid's Tale*, a story about women essentially becoming birthing machines. That's such a logical, dystopian extension of the universe and a way we could explain the absence of women in a part of the *Gears of War*

Opposite:
Gears of War screen grab

Above:
Shadow Complex logo

Universe. Humanity is at its end, and they have to keep producing soldiers, so women are essentially put on farms, "birthing crèches." Mike Capps liked the idea a lot and came up with the other half that the plot hinges on, a classic "Peter Parker/ Marvel does not save Uncle Ben twist," with Mike tossing in the idea that the women who are actually fighting in the war are barren and unable to have children. They can't produce soldiers. It was like boom, we've got it. It was a perfect idea. That's why you don't see many women in the *Gears* universe, because it is only the ones that cannot reproduce, and that is very many as most women can have babies. Mike Capps did a lot of writing for *Unreal Tournament*, I think mostly uncredited. He was ready to sink his teeth into comics as he is a big comic book fan and was really at the forefront of the movement to create a *Gears of War* comic. I asked him to co-write. Originally, I thought I would co-write with Cliff, but he was kind of hands off with the comic book. Mike was a great fit, since I wanted to co-write with someone from Epic. Mike wasn't just there "in name," he was seriously a co-writer for the story arc. We took turns splitting issues and he did a great job.

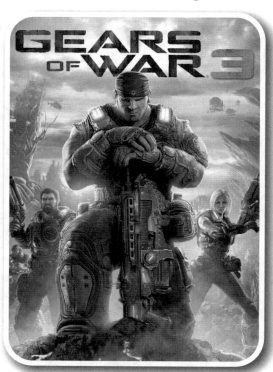

Veronese: It definitely is an exclamation point when you see that the president of Epic Games is a co-writer on the property.

Ortega: Yeah, it was really cool and he really brought his "A" game. He didn't coast, and he came up with some great little twists and lines. I was impressed; I told him he might be the best "writing president" in all of video games. I hope that's a compliment, because I think it is true.

Veronese: How does your process vary for writing a novel like ((Frequencies)), to a video game, to a science and technology article, to a comic script? Does the process vary at all?

Ortega: ((Frequencies)) was originally self-published. I initially came up with the concept in 1996. I wrote it in 1998 after about two years of on and off research while juggling three jobs to pay the bills, then spent one year of full on, forty hours plus a week writing. I finished the book exactly one year to the day I sat

down to write it at the forty-hours-plus a week pace. I put it out in the Summer of 1999. It was really big for me to get published in the 20th Century—then I can say I was published in both millennia, two different centuries. Also, if you remember all the Year 2000 hype—I was in Seattle with the World Trade Organization meeting riots on the horizon, and it was getting hot—you could feel a lot of stuff in the air. I felt like I need to get the work out as soon as possible. I went to a publisher, I had every bit of confidence that I could get a publisher, but it was going to take two years minimum to reach print. Why wait? I came from a hip hop music background, and I learned a lot about just doing things yourself. If you are willing to pull the weight and have a bit of business acumen, it's better—you get more control, more royalties, and you can move swifter and be more nimble, acting almost like a start-up company rather than a publisher. I just did that and got it out in 1999. I did a limited edition. They were numbered one to one thousand. Each book came wrapped in a comic bag with a limited edition bookmark and two postcards. I was very much comic-based in that sense, and the cover of that printing of ((Frequencies)) is very visual— just the logo, no writing. I think I was the first person to put out a novel with no writing on the cover, it just had a symbol. I was thinking at the time that everything was going to be touch screens and icons and logos soon, and, sure enough, that's the way it is ten years later. I signed all of the original editions, one through one thousand, then stuffed them in comic bags with the extras; it was so do-it-yourself. I didn't want stuff to fall out, so the comic bags were perfect. I made the price $19.99, fitting the year and the place in time we were in. I love playing with price numbers, the second edition that wasn't limited was priced at $17.76

All the work on the first edition really worked though. I wanted to make sure that everyone that purchased the limited edition got a "mint" copy, once again, coming from a

Above:
Gears of War #3 packaging art

comic background. I provided every bookstore in the area, since it was published locally, with an opened display copy of the book that readers could skim, so that the rest of the copies in bookstores could be kept mint and sealed. I remember one book store in Seattle that loved it—people just wanted to buy the wrapped book with no writing on the front, like it was forbidden.

Veronese: Seeing a book like that in the later 1990s, I would have jumped to buy it. The symbol combined with the wrapped nature and intrigue.

Ortega: And that was one of the biggest mistakes of the second printing. I did a forty-city book tour, with a huge print run of over twenty-thousand copies. We sold a lot of them, but we could have sold a million if we would have kept the blank cover with just the symbol. The publisher knew this is what I wanted, but they wanted to do something a little different with the release. I designed the symbol, and the symbol is ((Frequencies)). People gravitate toward it; it says everything about the novel without saying a word. I dropped the issue, and we went with a more traditional cover, but I was able to sneak a part of the symbol onto the more traditional cover. The book did well enough, but I know it could have been huge with something more similar to the original cover.

I am prepping now for what I call the "Omega Edition," doing one final edit, but not changing anything. It's been twelve years since the original release, and I'm getting ready to finish the sequel. I've been taking my time, but I've been waiting for the right time. I wanted to build my name up before I re-launched ((Frequencies)) and its universe. It's time now. My favorite author is Phillip K. Dick, and it took ten to fifteen years for people to get *Blade Runner*, and other books like *Neuromancer* and *Snow Crash*; some of these books just take a while. I think ((Frequencies)) is one of these books. It is so purely independent and so out of left field. It is just so different from normal novels; I didn't even follow a simple three act structure. It was a hyperlinked book printed in 1999, but now there are tablets and book readers, so I can do a lot more cool, unique things now that I couldn't do then. The edit is done, now it is just a matter of seeing how I want to left field. It is just so a matter of deciding the method. In a world of tablet readers, you just have to get with one graphic designer and you could have the book out overnight.

Veronese: What are some of the projects you are working on now?

Ortega: I just finished a gallery show in Los Angeles with artist Snakebite Cortez, who worked on the comic *The Red Star* under the name Byron Talmon (*The Red Star* was also adapted as a PS2 game). I wrote the stories the paintings were based on, and it's essentially like, "What if Superman was from Brazil?", "What if Wonder Woman was Incan?", and "What if Thor was Filipino?" We were doing a hip hop mash-up of archetypes, and I wrote a story, with Snakebite creating real, physical masks, fine art pieces, for each of the characters. That was my first foray into fine art. I call what we are doing "Warhol 2.0". We had a lot of celebrities and comic artists come out; it went off really well and we had a lot of fun.

Veronese: Could you tell us a little more about your hip hop background? It seems to permeate a lot of your work and they way you approach your work.

Ortega: The main work I did in that field was with a magazine in Seattle called *The Flavor*. We were one of the big indie magazines covering hip hop as it became America's and really, the world's, music and started to ascend in the mid 1990s. We did a lot of interesting stuff. We were the first to put Naz on the cover of a magazine and the first to put Biggie Smalls on a cover. It was a great time, especially to be on the indie level. We put on a five-dollar show for the second anniversary of *The Flavor*, and it featured Naz, Coolio, Supernatural, Kurious Jorge, and The Fugees. It was that era of hip hop. Five bucks for that lineup was crazy.

Veronese: That's at least a $150 ticket now, and only if you can get The Fugees in the same room now.

Ortega: That was a wonderful, really fun time in hip hop. Before the drama, before the Tupac and Biggie feud. I bowed out after a little bit; I just had to clear my head because it was so crazy. And it wasn't hip hop's fault; there was a lot of political stuff going on in the background.

Veronese: You mentioned working for Xbox for 4 years—what did you do during that time period?

Ortega: That was a wonderful learning experience; really a big part of the reason I've been so successful now with games, it really set me up. Eric Nylund (*Halo, Battlestar Galactica*) really brought me in at Microsoft, he acted sort of like my "recruiter." I knew him and his wife from the science-fiction book circuit. Microsoft had an open writer position, and he encouraged me to interview for it. I was looking to get into games. I had just finished working on the *Knight of the Old Republic* comic series for Dark Horse that was based on the game series from BioWare, and I was having a lot of fun being immersed in gaming again; I've been a gamer all my life.

The job was a lot of fun, I got to work on a lot of different intellectual properties and with a lot of different developers in the first two years and then I was exclusive to *Gears of War 2* for the last two years. My first credited game was the kids game *Viva Piñata*. I loved working on it—I have kids, the aesthetics are beautiful, and Rare is a great developer. I was also the liaison for 4Kids Entertainment, as they were launching the *Viva Piñata* cartoon at the same time as well. I got to keep track of continuity between the game and cartoon, acting like a franchise manager. Later I got to direct the voice-over sessions for the spin-off game, *Viva Piñata: Party Animals*. During this time period I also got to work with Hironobu Sakaguchi, the creator of the *Final Fantasy* series, on *Blue Dragon* and *Lost Odyssey* for the Xbox 360, and I got to co-direct the English version of *Lost Odyssey*. I briefly worked on Silicon Knights' *Too Human*, but I came on a little too late to make a large impact. I was lucky to be able to work on five shipped titles in two years.

Veronese: Comics, literary fiction, fine art, and video games—you have certainly covered a lot of ground.

Ortega: Cliff says I shouldn't call myself a writer anymore, that I should call myself a trans-media specialist. A lot people in comics seemed to think I was just a license writer/franchise writer. My first published comic book work was a Spider-Man story, and Ryan Sook did the art.

Veronese: It's hard to top that.

Ortega: Yeah, not bad at all coming out of the gate. I did a Batman story for *Legends of the Dark Knight* right before that, but it hasn't been printed. Dan Didio brought me on for that when he was just starting at DC Comics. I got to write *Star Wars*, *Star Trek*, Frazetta' *Death Dealer*, and *Battlestar Galactica* comic books soon after that, and a lot of people asked me if I felt creatively constrained working on franchise material. I didn't though—I got to write my

magnum opus, *((Frequencies))*, right out the gate and get it out of my system. I think a lot of people writing for a franchise have a novel they want to write or a story they really want to tell, and I did that early on. I started that way and did the first thing on my list first, and that allowed me to play around and have fun in a big sandbox of other universes and just try to tell the best stories I can within the parameters. I don't have to try to tell my story, as it has already been told and established. *((Frequencies))* is my baby, and I'll always take care of it and protect it. It's my main thing; I don't play around with it.

Writing for franchises is fun too. Franchise writing is like a puzzle where you are given ten words and you have to make the best story you can with those words. I've been blessed to work on a wide variety of work and with some great artists like Liam Sharp, Nat Jones, Simon Bisley, and a young Francis Manapul, one of my best friends to this day, who I co-created *Necromancer* with for Top Cow.

Veronese: How long was the script for *Gears of War 2*? Does it resemble something akin to a screenplay or a comic script?

Ortega: It was sort of part screenplay, part comic script. It's a combination; I kept calling it a "comic book screenplay" hybrid. It is definitely scripted similarly to a screenplay, but I've written a couple screenplays before, and admittedly, I'm not big on formatting in the Final Draft style. It overcomplicates the process, I just want to write. It's formatted a bit like a screenplay, but not rigorously. It's centered, dialogue is in the middle, but it is basically "left justified, middle dialogue." In some ways, it resembles more of a comic script, due to the way I write and the panel descriptions. It has more detail than a movie script, as directors don't typically like that. It's like a comic script in a way as I sort of wrote it in the style of telling the artist what to do. Greg Mitchell, the Cinematics Lead for *Gears of War 2* and 3, liked it a lot as he was able to practically shoot cinematics shot for shot from the script. He could definitely see the comic book writing experience in my background, with my insertion of angles and zooms in a script, but this is something that wouldn't work in a traditional screenplay as it would be over-direction.

Veronese: I don't think people realize how difficult it is to write a script with visual direction versus prose.

Ortega: I agree, but that's something I've always taken a knack too. With my first novel, ((Frequencies)), I remember a couple of people coming up to me on the book tour and saying, "I don't mean this to be rude or anything, but your novel reads more like a movie or a comic." I loved that—that's exactly what I wanted. I'm more of a visual storyteller at heart, I love visuals first and foremost. Almost any day, I would rather read a wordless comic than a novel.

Veronese: Are you playing any video games now?

Ortega: Right now I've been having fun playing a lot of older games with the kids, like *Legend of Zelda: Ocarina of Time*. My setup is pretty sweet; we have an antique wooden cabinet, about four feet high with a nice size flatscreen HDTV, not one of the crazy sixty inch ones, with a PS3 on the left and an Atari 2600 on the right. Those are the two consoles you can see from the front. It looks awesome—the wood paneling of the cabinet matches the Atari and the black on the Atari matches the PS3.

Veronese: You've got thirty years of video gaming lined up from left to right.

Ortega: It's my original machine and my current favorite. I have had two to three consoles from every generation of gaming; I've been a gamer all my life.

The current setup is a lot of fun. I've been playing a lot of Atari 2600 games with the kids, and it's helped me with the rise of app games as it has reminded me of some of the basic game mechanics; mechanics that can still be applied to a current generation game like *Gears of War 3*. The last really recent game I've bought and played through was *Heavy Rain*. It was genius. It's the beta version of what's to come—when the 2.0 version of that style of game comes out, it's going to be amazing. That's the only game my wife and I have played through together.

Veronese: My wife wouldn't let me play it unless she was in the room—she didn't want to miss any part of the story.

Ortega: I would let my wife take the controller and play through the fight scenes, and then, just before things got ugly, grab the controller back and win the fight. The controls are so intuitive she would just be able to pick it up. Some of the best fight scenes I've ever seen in a video game—so dramatic. Combined with the story, it's the next step in interactive entertainment. I've been waiting to see something like *Heavy Rain*, and it's definitely my favorite recent game, just from a pure ambition standpoint. It has replay ability too—my wife wants to play through it again to see how different choices affected the outcome of the story.

Opposite:
Viva Piñata: Party Animals promotional art

Below:
Gears of War screenshot

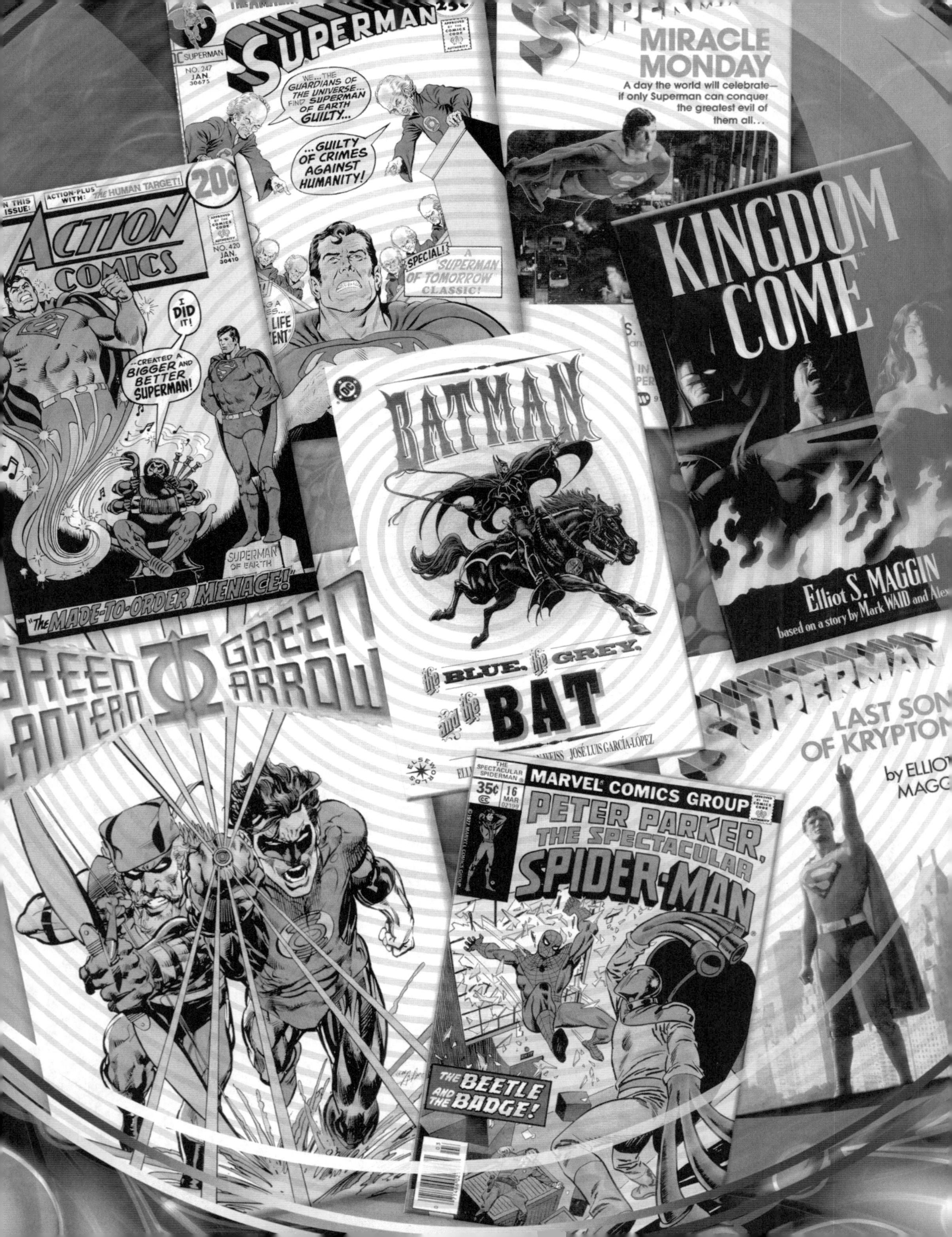

SUPERMAN
NO. 247 JAN. 30675
25¢
WE... THE GUARDIANS OF THE UNIVERSE... FIND SUPERMAN OF EARTH GUILTY...
...GUILTY OF CRIMES AGAINST HUMANITY!
SPECIAL! A "SUPERMAN OF TOMORROW" CLASSIC!
MIRACLE MONDAY
A day the world will celebrate—if only Superman can conquer the greatest evil of them all...
IN THIS ISSUE:
ACTION-PLUS WITH: THE HUMAN TARGET!
20¢
ACTION COMICS
NO. 420 JAN. 30410
I DID IT!
...CREATED A BIGGER AND BETTER SUPERMAN!
SUPERMAN OF EARTH
"The MADE-TO-ORDER MENACE!"
KINGDOM COME
Elliot S. MAGGIN
based on a story by Mark WAID and Alex
BATMAN
the BLUE, the GREY, and the BAT
JOSÉ LUIS GARCÍA-LÓPEZ
ELSEWORLDS
GREEN LANTERN GREEN ARROW
SUPERMAN
LAST SON OF KRYPTON
by ELLIOT MAGG
THE SPECTACULAR SPIDERMAN
MARVEL COMICS GROUP
35¢ 16 MAR 02199
PETER PARKER, THE SPECTACULAR SPIDER-MAN
THE BEETLE AND THE BADGE!

Elliot S! Maggin

Teacher, programmer, novelist, consultant for Kaiser Permanente, California House of Representatives hopeful, comic book writer—what can Elliot S! Maggin not do? Maggin is best known in comic circles for a fifteen-year stint on Superman, where he created Superboy-Prime and had a chance meeting with Jeph Loeb that sparked both of their careers.

Maggin's Superman stories and vision of the DC Universe is credited by many as basis for the timeless DC mini-series *Kingdom Come*, a series for which Maggin wrote the novelization. Maggin also wrote teleplays for *Spider-Man*, *X-Men*, and *Batman: The Animated Series*. Maggin was lucky enough to be around Atari in its brightest days, and he provides some very interesting insights into the company's inner workings.

Keith Veronese: When did you work for Atari? In what capacities were you with the company?

Elliot S! Maggin: I was a consultant with Atari's home computer division from around 1980 until early in 1984. My roles varied, but I was never on their payroll.

Veronese: How did your work in video games come about?

Maggin: I got a call in New Hampshire sometime early in 1980 from Joe Orlando, who was an editor at DC Comics at the time. He asked me—and he sounded either mysterious or uncertain, I'm not sure which—what my consulting rate was. I had no idea, so I made something up and he said okay. Warner Communications had just bought Atari and they were looking for sources of synergy between their acquisition and their newly adopted sister companies. Somebody in marketing—it was Brenda Laurel, who became a good friend

Opposite: (clockwise)
Action Comics #420, Superman #247, Superman Miracle Monday novel, *Kingdom Come, Superman: Last Son of Krypton* novel, *The Spectacular Spider-Man #16, Green Lantern/Green Arrow,* and *Batman: The Blue, the Grey, and the Bat*

Above:
Atari 800 advertisement

and then got relatively famous—asked around at DC Comics if they knew anyone with a background vaguely involved with both fantasy and education and they came up with me. I'm not sure whether I was writing any comic books on a regular basis at the time, but I think I wasn't and started up again soon afterward. So I went down to New York and met with Joe Orlando, Jenette Kahn, and Brenda Laurel. Brenda had a whole Atari 800 system shipped to my house and told me she wanted me to learn everything I could about the computer and figure out what we could do with it. I spent the next two weeks learning BASIC and wrote a long memo about something I called "interactive fiction," which is something I'm convinced to this day that I invented. Pretty quickly I learned Logo and 6502 Assembly languages and I've been picking up software and programming language like barnacles ever since. Also, I got pretty good at a game called *Star Raiders*.

The first project I did with Atari was something that didn't pan out quite the way we planned. Everything I did with Atari didn't pan out quite the way we planned. I came up with a scenario and a bunch of characters called *Star Raiders*, after the Atari game, and wrote a series of four stories that were supposed to be packaged and

Above:
Star Raiders packaging

Below:
Star Raiders graphic novel

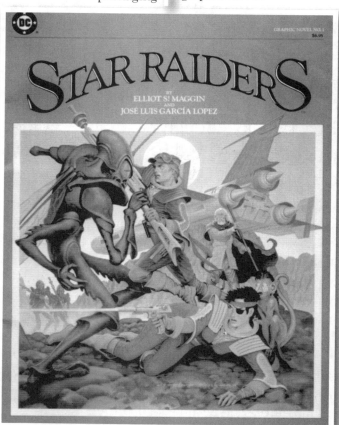

distributed with the next four Atari computer game ROM cartridges. The idea was that you buy all four games and you get the whole story. For some reason Atari couldn't coordinate their release schedule tightly enough to guarantee the release of all four story installments reliably, so the project got canned. Meanwhile, I had written and José Luis García-López had drawn—actually painted in acrylics—all four stories. So someone thought it'd be a good idea to cram them together and bring them out as a single graphic novel. They didn't work as a single story appended one after the other, so I took Jose's already painted pages, reordered and rearranged them, and made up a new story to fit the new format. It looked great. I'm not enamored with the story. I didn't realize it didn't hang together any better than it had before, until it came out on the stands. It was DC's first graphic novel, though, and it was loosely based on the Atari game.

Veronese: What were some of the games and concepts you worked on for Atari?

Maggin: Meanwhile, I was in a position to come up with something—anything—new to do with Atari, which was the bigass corporate superstar of the moment. A proposal I wrote for them with the idea that DC would be involved was something I eventually called *Timegate*, a transponder-and-modem-based game series that was way too far ahead of its time. Remember Snapper Carr? The Justice League teenage sidekick from the Sixties? Well my idea for synergy between Atari and DC was to make Justice League adventures interactive, and to turn each reader or player into Snapper Carr. The JLA headquarters at the time was a satellite in geosynchronous orbit where someone was on duty at all times. The premise of the game series was that the only four civilians in constant contact with the Justice League of America satellite were (1) the President of the United States, (2) the Secretary-General of the United Nations, (3) the Chief Justice of the World Court at The Hague and (4) the kid playing the game of the month. I wrote an extended scenario for the first game, called *Artthief*. The premise was that Luthor had stolen the great art treasures of the world and hidden them somewhere in the solar system. I outlined multiple plotlines and multiple outcomes, based on the decisions the player would make on deploying JLA members and resources. It was just a beautiful thing to behold, and my favorite thing about it was the fantasy conceit that the player was sitting

Above:
Snapper Carr from *Who's Who in the DC Universe*

Below:
Atari logo

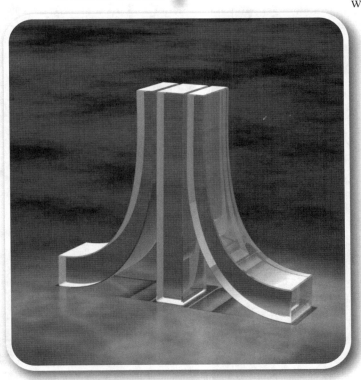

at home, in contact with the JLA satellite 22,300 miles above the equator, when in real-life the subscriber was in fact in touch with a Warner Communications transponder beaming down the premises of a JLA game to him or her once a month.

For reasons I can't remember or maybe was never aware of, DC's involvement with the project just petered away. So a friend from New Hampshire and I came up with something we called *Timegate*, an interactive game series whose plotlines were different from those of my Justice League series, but whose mechanics were pretty much the same. I suspect the idea eventually evolved into something about some person named Carmen Somethingorother. But it was my idea first. Honest.

The problem with the premises of what I came up with was that they were too tied up with satellite transmission—eminently do-able at the time, and that was the sort of thing they were paying me to come up with, after all—but there just wasn't the installed base of potential customers with modem access to make the product economically practical. Nobody had Internet at the time except generals and scientists. It was ten years before even I was wired to the rest of the hive-mind, and another five or eight years before the rest of the world began to catch up.

Veronese: Could you talk about the Atari "culture" during the time you were affiliated with the company?

Maggin: I thought of putting together a book—sort of like the *New Machine* book Tracy Kidder wrote back then—called *Atari: The Rise and Fall of a Corporate Superstar.* I had—if not a front seat—a pretty good mezzanine view of the whole process.

Atari culture was very brash and macho in those days. It seemed everyone within the home computer division (there were three divisions: coin-op, game machine, and home computers) hung out at this big bar in Sunnyvale a block or two from the division offices. Olivia Newton-John's song "Let's Get Physical" was really big in those days, so this bar decided to sponsor an annual "Most Physical Female" contest. The Atari gay/lesbian employees' organization decided to sponsor an annual "Most Metaphysical Female" contest. It cracked everyone up, but I'm not sure whether there was a second annual version of either contest.

People did business over lunch and over drinks. The post of

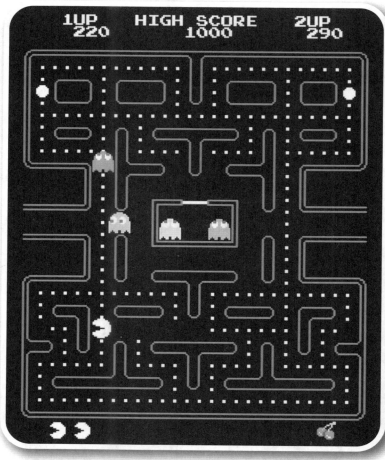

Above:
Pac-Man
Below:
Dig Dug

Opposite:
Free Cell

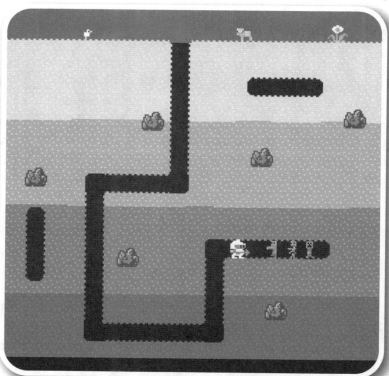

president of the various divisions was a revolving door, as were the posts of the department chiefs. I don't know whether that was an Eighties corporate thing or specifically an Atari thing, but it seemed to me Atari was basically analogous to New Hampshire government at the time. Both were essentially banana republics, little operations swimming boldly among predators, a lot of fast-and-loose money surfacing for one thing or other every once in awhile, and run by a succession of strongmen heavy on the personality and lacking a bit on substance.

For a while, I kind of resented it when Atari evaporated into the ozone before really getting anything I'd done out the door, but that was standard in the industry during its birthing traumas. I made friends in those days with a guy named Alan Kay, a young scientist who had been involved with the fabled Xerox PARC and was a consultant with Atari along with me. He and the guys in the Xerox PARC group had pretty much invented the premises, protocols, and interfaces of what became the personal computer years later.

The problem was that Xerox as a company opted out of the personal computer game early, leaving behind all these people and their intellectual capital to flap in the wind like Soviet nuclear scientists. So everything went out to the nearest lucky bidder: people and ideas alike. Out of that came Apple and Atari and Tandy and Microsoft and Commodore (remember Commodore?) and Adobe and Macromedia and a slew of other competitors. Most eventually got eaten by one another like a nest of pythons, and the fans and adherents of the survivors argue to this day over who first came up with this interface or that standard function or the other cliché. So I don't really worry about it any more—other than to tell anyone who asks that I invented interactive fiction. But so did Brenda, for that matter, and probably a slew of other people. Comfort comes in the realization that ultimately the Universe wastes exactly nothing.

I just realized: I think maybe the Universe wasted 8-tracks and Betamaxes.

Veronese: How would you define "interactive fiction"? How did the idea come about?

Maggin: Interactive fiction is any coherent plot line whose progress is either driven or influenced by the act of reading or experiencing it. The idea came about pretty much through the availability of the medium to convey it. The plan for Atari was to give me a computer and a crash course in BASIC programming and to see what I thought they could do with their consumer-oriented machinery. I'm not sure how new the idea of interactive fiction was, but I did write a long memo giving it a name and proclaiming it a "new form."

Veronese: What was the writing process like for interactive fiction? You have a passion for it, obviously, but writing branching story points dependent on a player's decisions (a format used extensively in popular modern role-playing games like *Mass Effect* and *Star Wars: Knights of the Old Republic*) must make for a great deal of work, especially when writing dialogue strands.

Maggin: To write in this form, you use a lot of 3-by-5 cards. I'm not sure any system more sophisticated than handwritten notes has been developed that will deal with it effectively. It's similar to writing a crossword puzzle, I suppose. You have to start with a beginning, figure out how many possible endings you want, and devise the most circuitous and interwoven way you can to get to each of those endings. When you reread a conventional story or a script in order to edit a final draft, you have to look at the piece as a coherent whole, evaluating how well one event or scene leads to the next. With an interactive story, unless it's profoundly simplistic, you have to do the same for every plot line you can determine, and make lots and lots of notes.

Veronese: What programming languages do you know? Are they primarily self taught?

Maggin: All the programming languages I know are self-taught. I know BASIC pretty well—and I even met John Kemeni a thousand years ago. He sent a contribution to my campaign for Congress. I told him I was a big fan of his language but all I really wanted to talk about was Einstein. I have a passing knowledge of 6502-Assembly, a pretty good understanding of FORTH and LOGO (mostly in the form of Atari PILOT), and I tried to learn MUMPS once but I lost patience. What I'm really pretty adept at are a few of the online markup languages and their attendants: HTML, SQL, JavaScript, ColdFusion, PHP, and just enough Java to be dangerous.

Veronese: Do you play video games now?

Maggin: Video games now? *Zaxxon* came out when I was in my late 30s and I realized my reflexes weren't near what they were when I was a big fan of *Pac-Man* and *Dig Dug*. I went on Jeopardy not long afterward and found my thumb continually slipping off the button against my will. I spend a bizarre amount of time online these days playing *Free Cell* (involves more thinking and less reacting), but the newer arcade games are pretty much an alien landscape. I've dabbled in computer-based role-playing games, especially when I was working for DC and TSR, but I don't really keep up. It's sort of like building a desktop PC: I do it about every ten years, just to make sure I'm up-to-date at least for a moment or two.

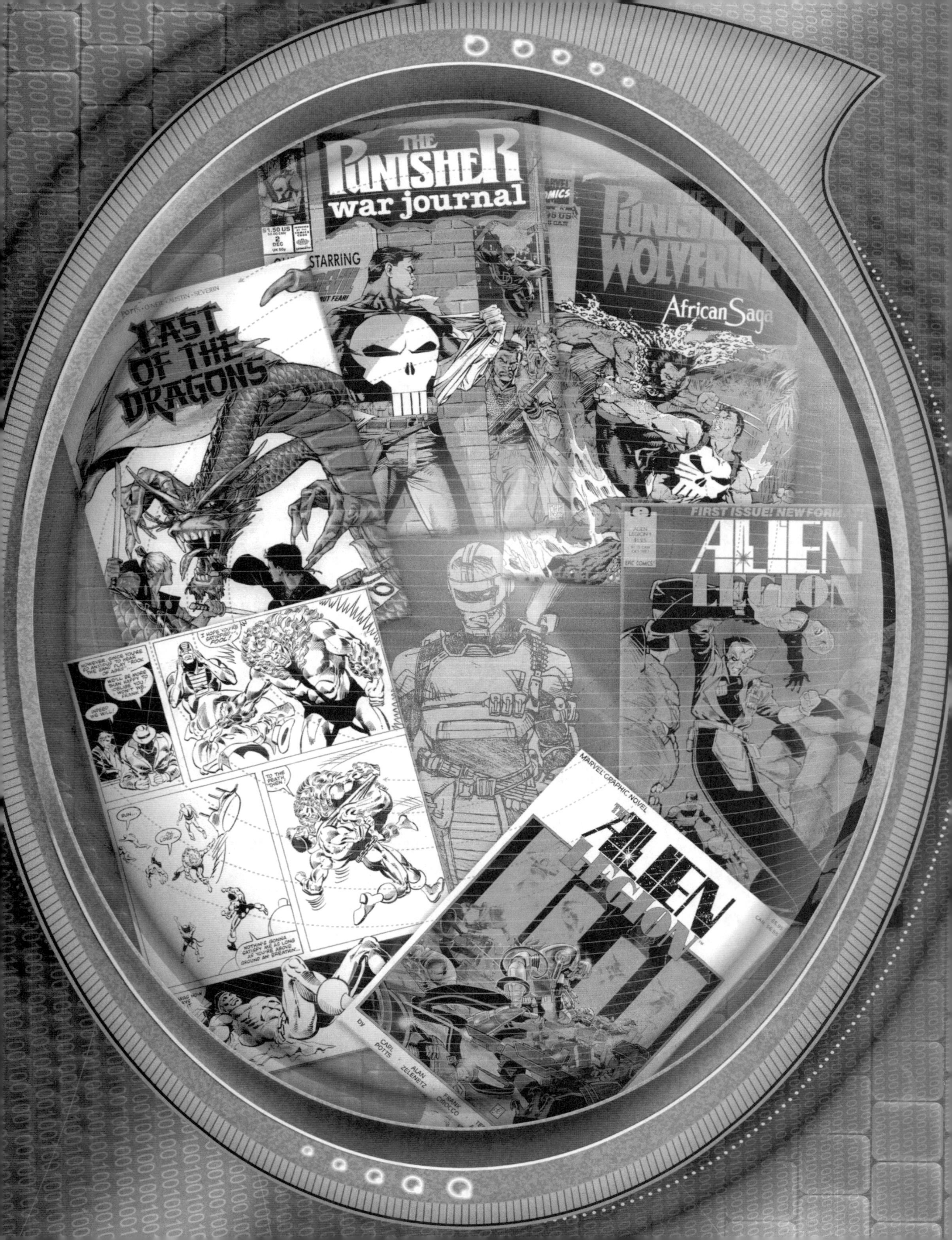
THE PUNISHER
war journal
STARRING
THE PUNISHER
WOLVERINE
African Saga
LAST OF THE DRAGONS
FIRST ISSUE! NEW FORMAT
ALIEN LEGION
EPIC COMICS
I HOPE YOU'RE SATISFIED, FOOL!
INDEED WE WILL!
TO THE DEATH, THEN!
RUN...
NOTHIN'S GONNA SATISFY ME AS LONG AS YOU'RE ABOVE GROUND AN' BREATHIN'...
MARVEL GRAPHIC NOVEL
THE ALIEN LEGION
by
CARL POTTS
ALAN ZELENETZ
FRANK CIROCCO

Carl**Potts**

Carl Potts picked up his first job in comic books performing fill-in and background work for an issue of DC Comics' *Richard Dragon: Kung Fu Fighter* alongside Jim Starlin and Alan Weiss. Potts spent several years at Neal Adams' Continuity Studios before taking an editorial position at Marvel Comics in 1983.

At Marvel, Carl Potts co-created *Alien Legion* (recently licensed by Disney for a movie) and directed the handling of the Punisher in the mid-1980s, transforming the character from a guest-star to leading man. This work withstanding, Potts' biggest impact on the industry stems from the role he played in developing the early careers of Arthur Adams and Jim Lee, legends in the comic book industry.

Keith Veronese: Your work in comics has a distinct legacy, especially in light of Marvel's rise in the mid-to-late 1980s and early 1990s under talent (Jim Lee, Whilce Portacio, Scott Williams) you guided as an editor. How did you go from an embedded editor to working in the video game industry?

Carl Potts: Almost by accident, I was an early pioneer in the home computer game business. In the early '80s the Jim Henson Company hired me to provide the art for an interactive game based on their *Dark Crystal* movie—a "choose your own adventure" style game. I had to input the very simplified art into an early Apple.

Veronese: That is extremely interesting—that's one of the earliest reference to video games I have come across thus far from someone within the comic industry. How did you get involved in the home computer game boom? Was it a part of your educational background?

Potts: I got involved with *Dark Crystal* by accident. If I remember correctly someone at Henson's contacted Marvel to see if anyone there

Opposite: (clockwise)
Last of the Dragons Graphic Novel, *The Punisher War Journal #2*, *The Punisher/Wolverine: African Saga*, *Alien Legion #1, The Alien Legion* Graphic Novel and *Powerman and Iron Fist #84* interior page

Above: The Alien Legion Team

would be interested in working on the game. Somehow, even though I was doing very little work for Marvel at the time, my name was suggested. I played arcade video games quite a bit back then but had no personal computer experience at the time.

Veronese: What sort of input did you have on the art for the *Dark Crystal* video game? Did you do line art that was later converted to digital art, or did you do the actual digital art? Did you have any story input?

Potts: I drew simple line art on paper and then used a pen/tablet input device to put it into the

Apple. Even as simple as the work was, I had to make the art simpler to take up less memory. Shortly after that, I went on staff at Marvel and didn't really keep up with computers or computer games until sometime in the early '90s. Marvel's owners in the early/mid '90s were in the process of driving the company into bankruptcy. Marvel went through several waves of massive layoffs. It looked the end was approaching, so I kept an eye open for future career opportunities. Electronic entertainment was an area I considered. When the founder of VR-1 Entertainment, an online entertainment company based in Boulder, Colorado, asked me to head their digital comics program, I accepted. VR-1's main thrust was massively multiplayer online games and I gradually got involved in that arena. VR-1 produced games across a range of categories including 3-D vehicular combat, turn-based strategy

games, small Shockwave games—even an "audio MUD." Their most successful title, *Fighter Ace*, was online for over 10 years, only recently shutting down.

Veronese: An audio MUD would be really cool— you could play that in the car.

Potts: The game, *Crossroads*, had a 360-degree audio environment. I don't believe it ever got released here. It may have been up in South Korea at one point.

Veronese: Were the digital comics at VR-1

Above: (top to bottom)
Screenshot of *The Dark Crystal* game
Gelfling Adventure packaging/disk
Opposite: (top to bottom)
Fighter Ace screenshot
UltraCorps screenshot

Entertainment to be licensed ones or new properties?

Potts: Most of the comics were originals created by the VR-1 staff. The *Megabot* comic eventually evolved into the *UltraCorps* game. I did have three new action adventure comics in development when the plug got pulled on digital comics at VR-1. Some of the comic pros I had working on them included Dan Abnett and Andy Lanning, Chuck Dixon, D.G. Chichester, Alcatena, and Barry Crain. We did briefly license one kid's property from Tom Mason at Mainbrain and Disney asked us to produce a 3-D *Gargoyles* episode.

Veronese: What do you think is missing for the digital comics medium to really take off? They seem to be excellent attractors for new readers, especially with licensed properties, but it seems like the typical comic reader is clinging to their pulp and paper.

Potts: These are just a few glaring problems seen in the past with digital comics. Reading comics on a horizontal rectangle monitor only works for comics that are made for that format. So, putting re-purposed comics content on the web, with a fixed horizontal monitor, created an awkward reading experience. Also, the bandwidth created a wait-for-the-content

experience that was frustrating for the reader. At the time when we started working on digital comics, there were no portable devices that had decent resolution. The final problem we came across was that it was not clear if duplicating the page-turning reading experience of a print comic was what the audience wanted, or if they wanted semi-animated comics with soundtracks and interactivity, morphing a comic book into a sort of a high-end animatic.

Technology has overcome a lot of these obstacles. With the current bandwidth available, tablets (with sufficient resolution) being in the hands of consumers and the capabilities of Flash, I think digital comics are finally going to take off. I'm still not sure if the comic book industry has determined if it wants to provide comics online comics that emulate reading print or if consumers want animated productions. Perhaps there is room for both.

Veronese: What video game projects did you work on?

Potts: *Dark Crystal* and *UltraCorps* (a galactic conquest turn-based strategy game) got to the market. *UltraCorps* was originally on Microsoft's Gaming Zone but is currently owned by Steve Jackson Games.

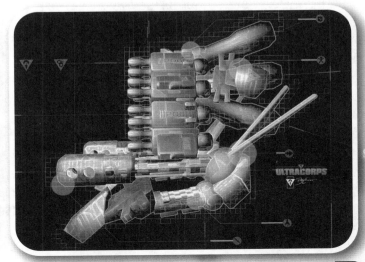

Veronese: How long did you work on *Dark Crystal* and *Ultracorps*?

Potts: I'm guessing less than 2 months on *Dark Crystal*, and *Ultra-Corps* was mostly a matter of team/project management for me. The game's two creators did the bulk of the creative work. I guess that took less than a year. A lot of the 3-D assets had already been created for the *Megabot* comic.

I also worked on the game designs for a *Legion of Super-Heroes* turn-based strategy game, a fishing tournament strategy game, a 3-D online game based on *Men in Black*, and a few others.

Some of my favorites were not based on licensed entities, like a concept we had for a game called *Airship Inferno*. It was a MMO 3-D vehicular combat game. We did a "trailer" for it but I can't seem to locate it. The setting was a Victorian/Steampunk era where players had to maneuver their airships and do battle around a fog- and smog-covered London. Whenever the player's ship cannons fired, you had to manage the recoil effect on your ship. As you used up powder and ammunition, the weight of your ship decreased so you had to manage your hot air produc-

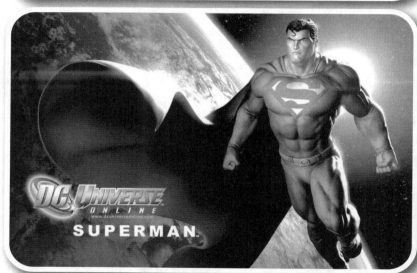

tion and retention (ballast too). I also worked on a futuristic scenario for the mechanics of the game.

Another game I worked on was *Shark Week*. It was a 3-D MMO game we pitched to Discovery Channel in correlation with their annual *Shark Week* programming. Players would pick the species of shark they wanted to be (be it a whale shark, hammerhead, tiger, mako, mega mouth, bull, nurse, great white, etc.), with their choice of species affecting the player's speed, target prey, feeding techniques, endurance, preferred habitat, and migration routes. The players and their shark avatar had to survive and thrive by getting enough food while avoiding being eaten by other players or AI orcas while at the same time staying away from health level sapping polluted areas and avoid being caught by AI fishermen on the look out for shark fin soup!

Veronese: Was the *Legion of Super-Heroes* strategy game released? Was the *Men in Black* game a movie tie-in or a project that came later?

Potts: No, the *Legion of Super-Heroes* game didn't get past the game design stage. It was to be built with the same turn-based, database-driven strategy game engine created previously for *UltraCorps*. *Men in Black* was not a direct movie tie in.

Veronese: You are the first industry professional I've encountered that has experience in game design, as most comics professionals have worked solely on story/art aspects. Could you give a little background into the actual "game design" process? What were some of the more enjoyable parts about working on game mechanics and game design? What are some of the challenges?

Potts: Challenges inherent in game design include making sure the game play is compelling for extended periods of play and for repeat players. You have to balance game elements so that players attain greater abilities and or powers with experience, but not in ways that make it too difficult for new players to get established in the game world. If that happens, experienced players can go newbie hunting.

In 2001, DC Comics asked me to put together a pitch to win support from the Warner Brothers brass for the development of a massively multiplayer DC Universe game. The pitch was successful. After several fits and starts, Sony Online Entertainment (with my former VR-1 comrade John Blakely in charge) produced the game *DC Universe Online*. Outside of the initial pitch, I had no involvement in the game's development.

Veronese: What went into creating the pitch for what eventually became *DC Universe Online*? Were there any challenges you initially foresaw? This was arguably the most awaited game of the past decade, and it's really great that it hasn't disappeared into the ether, as I'm sure there were several points where the project could have dissolved.

Potts: I wrote and storyboarded a scenario that showed how a player would enter the DC Universe game world as a civilian and later experience situation that would allow them to gain powers and interact with each other and iconic DC characters. I hired Will Rosado to do the finished art based on the storyboards. This artwork was put into an animatic and shown to the Warner execs as part of a larger presentation on the potential of a DC Universe game.

Veronese: What are you working on right now?

Potts: In recent years I've served as creative director for NY-area companies. Earlier this year I sold my *Alien Legion* screenplay to Bruckheimer/Disney. I'm currently producing a new *Alien Legion* mini-series for Dark Horse. Dark Horse is publishing a series of *Alien Legion* collections in their Omnibus format. Two volumes are out already.

I'd talked to VR-1 about a massively multiplayer online *Alien Legion* game when I was there but when I began actively trying to set it up for a film deal, I wanted to keep all of the ancillary rights intact, making the property more attractive to potential film companies.

I've been approached many times by paper RPG game companies about doing an *Alien Legion* game, but it seemed like a tremendous amount of work for very little return.

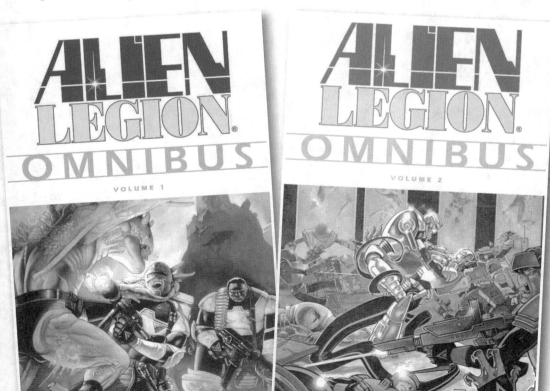

Opposite:
DC Universe Online promotional art

Above:
Volumes from the *Alien Legion* Omnibus collection

STAR WARS
KUNG FU
YOU KARATE KILLERS WANTED A SHOWDOWN--
--NOW YOU'VE GOT IT!
MARVEL COMICS
I'VE DONE IT!! I'VE DEFEATED THE INVADERS!
ALL NEW!
GHOST RIDER
A LEGEND IS BORN!
Prince Namor, THE
NEW! FIRST TIME IN COMIC-BOOK FORM!
CONAN THE BARBARIAN
15¢ 1 OCT
MARVEL COMICS GROUP
TO THE DEATH!
DOCTOR STRANGE
12¢ 177 FEB
DR. STRANGE
ATARI FORCE
30¢ 3 AUG
MARVEL COMICS GROUP
EDGAR RICE BURROUGHS'
Tarzan
AMAZING ADVENTURES
MARVEL COMICS GROUP
6P. 16 JAN
AMAZING ADVENTURES FEATURING
THE BEAST
YOUR STRENGTH COULD NEVER MATCH THE JUGGERNAUT!
YOU WERE DOOMED FROM THE START!
SPIDER-MAN
101 OCT
STILL 15¢
THE AMAZING SPIDER-MAN
MARVEL COMICS GROUP

Roy**Thomas**

A name synonymous with comic books, Roy Thomas was one of the first writers to define himself outside of Stan Lee in the early Sixties, writing *X-Men*, *Sgt. Fury*, *Avengers*, and a plethora of other series. Thomas became Editor-in-Chief of Marvel Comics in 1971, but continued to write full-time and playing a role in the creation of Marvel icons *Iron Fist* and *Ghost Rider*.

One of Thomas' greatest achievements as Editor-in-Chief of Marvel was bringing *Conan the Barbarian* and other licensed properties to Marvel. *Conan* was also written by Roy Thomas, and sold nearly as many copies as *Amazing Spider-Man* at the time, consistently beating Marvel stalwarts like *Avengers* and *Fantastic Four* in sales.

Roy Thomas championed Marvel to adapt George Lucas' *Star Wars* after securing the initial rights for free, a shrewd move that arguably saved Marvel Comics from financial collapse in the late 1970s.

Thomas moved into an editorial position with DC Comics in the early 1980s, where he often worked with fellow writer/editor Gerry Conway (the duo previously collaborated to create *Man-Thing*). Conway and Thomas teamed up in the creation of *Atari Force* and several joint Atari/DC ventures under the parent company Time Warner in the 1980s. Roy Thomas is still quite active in the world of comic books, editing *Alter Ego* magazine for TwoMorrows Publishing.

Keith Veronese: Did you interact much with Atari while working on *Swordquest*?

Roy Thomas: We had done a couple of things already. Gerry might remember things a little differently—he did a lot

Opposite:
Star Wars #1, Iron Fist #15, Marvel Premiere #30, Marvel Spotlight #5, Prince Namor, The Sub-Mariner #8, Conan The Barbarian #1, Dr. Strange #177, Atari Force #2, The Amazing Spider-man #101, Amazing Adventures #16, and Tarzan #3

Above:
Issues of Roy Thomas' *Alter Ego*

more on these projects that I did. We were sort of partners, but he did the vast majority of the work. At the time we had only done *Atari Force*, and we had ideas for a couple of other things, and then they (Atari) came up with the idea for *Swordquest*. Atari flew us up and we worked with some of the executives and engineers, mostly engineers, the people who would be preparing the game. Three or four of us sat around and talked about the game for a couple of hours, and this is where Gerry and I came up with the Earth, Fire, Air, Water part of *Swordquest*. Atari already had the idea to split up the project into four games, but we came up with the element idea.

Veronese: What was the Atari campus like?

Thomas: It was beautiful; it was like a little college campus. There was a beautiful building made of glass with sweeping stairs on both sides, with a very ultra-modern look for the early 1980s. They had a lot of extra facilities—one of the main things I remember is the gymnasium, a good way to keep in shape after staring at a computer all day. The Atari campus had a really nice layout—a kind of "homey" place. It looked like the perfect place to go to work. They were trying to create an environment that made people feel proud to be working there. The campus also reflects the fact that they were making a lot of money at the time.

Veronese: Did Gerry and yourself have any input on the clues put into the *Swordquest*?

Thomas: Gerry probably

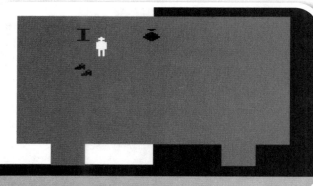

talked to them a little bit more—he was more into computers than I was, but as far as I remember, Atari handled most of the clues. Our part was in producing the comic—we may have communicated a little, but I don't remember. I don't recall an awful lot of coordination there. I don't think I've even seen all three of the published *Swordquest* books.

Veronese: Supposedly there is art for the unreleased fourth book floating around.

Thomas: Gerry and I split the plotting and dialogue, so I'm not sure how far we got on the fourth book, but if there's art existing, then there's a script, so we got farther than I thought. I printed a page from *Swordquest* in *Alter Ego #100*, and I thought I wrote it, but the more I looked at it, I thought the phrasing was off, it wasn't like me. Gerry and I didn't work together on things, in general, if I wrote a plot, he would glance over it, but we really didn't have much input on each other's work. It was simpler to work separately than waste our

Above: (top to bottom)
Swordquest: Earthworld packaging art

Swordquest: Earthworld screenshot

Atari Age #3

Opposite above:
Swordquest two-page ad

Opposite below: (left to right)
Swordquest contest advertisement

Swordquest $25,000 gold chalice advertisement

time duplicating each other.

Veronese: Was it odd to be working with such talented DC artists (George Pérez, Ross Andru, Gil Kane, and more) on a project that a lot of regular DC readers might not see?

Thomas: It was definitely an outreach effort, something trying to widen the fan base of comics by reaching new people. Atari wouldn't let us get too far out—we couldn't get too risqué or show much violence. It had to be a kind of "white bread" sword-and-sorcery story. George drew it beautifully, but we really couldn't put a lot of guts into it. Also, George would do this beautifully detailed artwork, and then it was printed in mini-comic form, so you would lose the detail. It's a real shame those books have never been collected and reprinted in a larger format as a four-issue set—with Pérez artwork, I would think there would be a market for them.

I liked the idea of working with Atari—I don't remember if we got regular rates or better than regular pay, but we did good work and got to work

with Atari before the implosion. Was it true that people were searching for the "treasure" offered as part of the fourth game?

*[**Author's note:** The Swordquest series offered lavish gold and diamond encrusted prizes for players who solved riddles that involved the game and comic, with some of these buried treasures advertised to have values in the $25,000 range.]*

Veronese: I haven't heard that story, but I wouldn't be surprised if people got shovels out and started digging. From what I understand, everyone who was in the running for the final *Swordquest* prize after solving the puzzles accompanying the previous games received a payment of $2500 from Atari as "consolation" money since the fourth game and comic never came out.

Thomas: I didn't get $2500, I don't think Gerry did either (laughs). That would have been a rather sizable payment back in those days; I would have probably remembered it.

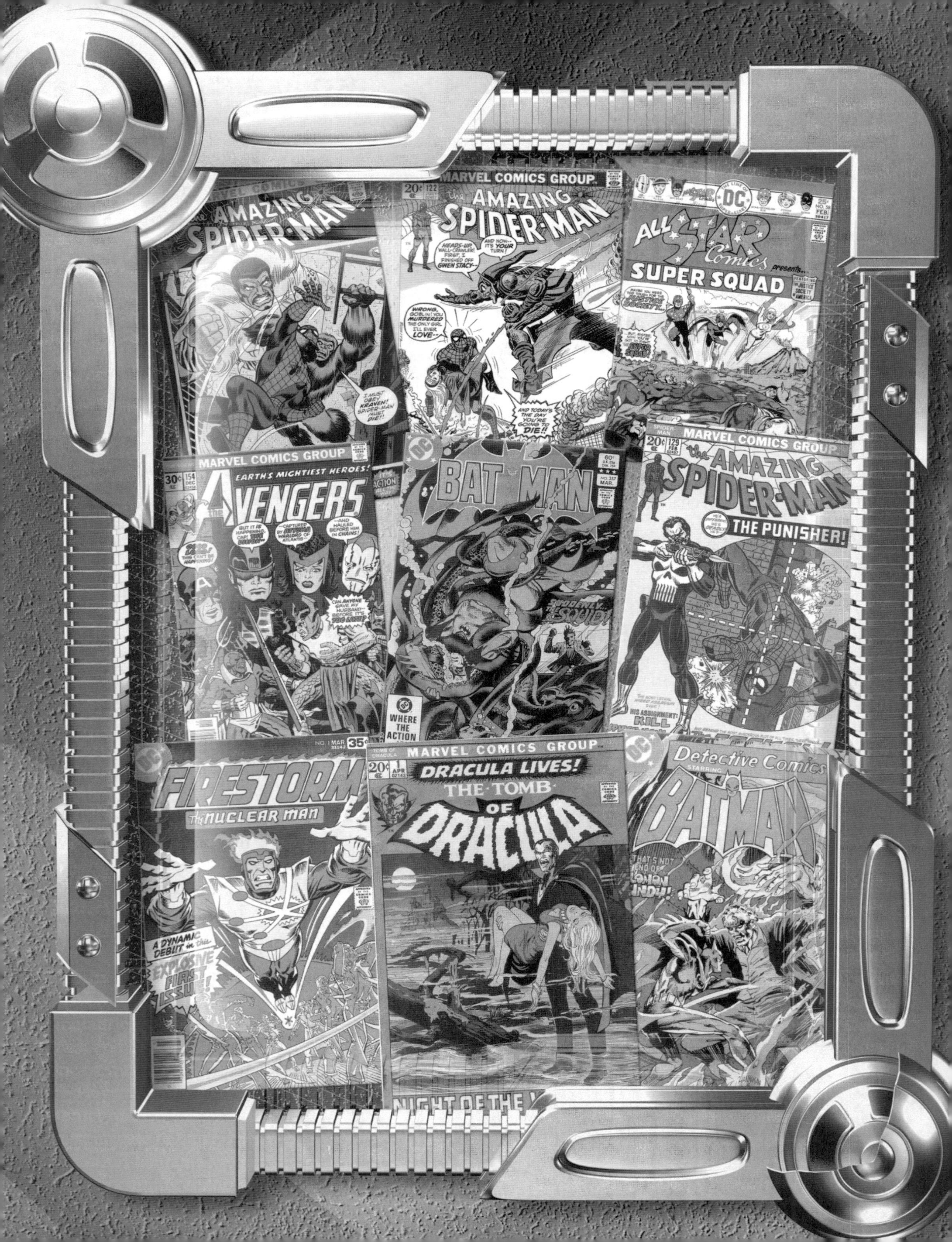

MARVEL COMICS
the AMAZING SPIDER-MAN
I MUST OBEY KRAVEN! SPIDER-MAN MUST DIE!!
MARVEL COMICS GROUP
20¢ 122
the AMAZING SPIDER-MAN
HEADS-UP, WALL-CRAWLER! FIRST, I FINISHED OFF GWEN STACY--
AND NOW-- IT'S YOUR TURN!
WRONG, GOBLIN! YOU MURDERED THE ONLY GIRL I'LL EVER LOVE--
AND TODAY'S THE DAY YOU'RE GOING TO DIE!!
DC
ALL STAR Comics presents...
SUPER SQUAD
FEATURING THE JUSTICE SOCIETY OF AMERICA
MARVEL COMICS GROUP
30¢ 154
EARTH'S MIGHTIEST HEROES!
the AVENGERS
--AND HAULED BEFORE HIM IN CHAINS!
CAN ANYONE SAVE MY HUSBAND-- BEFORE IT'S TOO LATE?
BATMAN
60¢
NO. 257 MAR.
WHERE THE ACTION IS
MARVEL COMICS GROUP
20¢ 129 FEB
the AMAZING SPIDER-MAN
THE PUNISHER!
NO. 1 MAR 35¢
FIRESTORM
THE NUCLEAR MAN
A DYNAMIC DEBUT in this EXPLOSIVE FIRST ISSUE!
MARVEL COMICS GROUP
20¢ 1 APR
DRACULA LIVES!
THE TOMB OF DRACULA
NIGHT OF THE
Detective Comics
STARRING
BATMAN

Gerry**Conway**

At the age of 19, Gerry Conway succeeded Stan Lee as the writer on *Amazing Spider-Man* with issue #111 and stayed on the title for just over three years. His tenure on *Amazing Spider-Man* continues to resonate thanks to the groundwork laid with the original Clone Saga, the death of Gwen Stacy, and the first appearance of the Punisher. Conway moved to DC Comics in the mid-1970s, where he help usher in the beginning of the Bronze Age with the revival of *All Star Comics* and the introduction of the popular Power Girl. At DC, Conway created Firestorm and also introduced Jason Todd and Killer Croc to the world.

In the early 1980s, Conway co-wrote the Ralph Bakshi and Frank Frazetta animated film *Fire and Ice* and the Arnold Schwarzenegger film *Conan the Destroyer* with fellow Marvel and DC superstar Roy Thomas. In the intervening years, Conway took on more television and film scripting duties, writing for *Matlock, Hercules: The Legendary Journeys,* and *The Huntress,* along with *Law and Order.*

Keith Veronese: You were involved in both the *Swordquest* and *Atari Force* projects. Were you involved with one more than the other? From talking to Roy Thomas, it sounds like you were more involved with *Atari Force.*

Gerry Conway: I don't know if I was involved with either projects more, but because of my background in computers, my interest was greater. I was a bit of a "proto-gamer" at the time,

Opposite:
Amazing Spider-Man #111, Amazing Spider-Man #122, All Star Comics #58, The Avengers #154, Batman #357, The Amazing Spider-Man #129, Firestorm #1, The Tomb of Dracula #1, and *Detective Comics #523,*

Above:
Fire and Ice movie poster

so I enjoyed the idea itself of working on projects for Atari and with the Atari people. Roy and I were already working together on other projects, so it made sense to work together on these. We were also the two main West Coast writers for DC at that point (with Atari's headquarters being in San Francisco, California).

Veronese: Because of its proximity, did you get to visit Atari often? What was the campus like?

Conway: We went up at least twice. We got a bunch of free video games and we got to see a few of their arcade games before they were released, which was cool. We got to see *Tempest* before it came out. We talked to the developers a bit. My general sense was that they weren't terribly interested in this, but that it was in an attempt by Warner Brothers, the parent company, to create some synergy between Atari and DC Comics. Jenette Kahn (DC Comics President at the time) was a primary component of this; it was primarily conceived as a marketing tool.

I don't consider the miniature *Atari Force* comic that was packaged with the Atari cartridges as representative of what I really wanted to do—it was a corporate work at the time, with nothing too extreme since we didn't really know who our audience was for that material. I created the separate *Atari Force* series for DC Comics later on, which was done out of enjoyment, for myself and for the readership in the comics medium. That material was much better established and conceived than the material we did earlier that was packaged with the video games.

Veronese: So the pack-in comics were seen mainly as a promotional tool to bring new readers to DC?

Conway: I don't know if anyone really understood what would come of it. At this point in the early 1980s, video games were very short, conceptually.

You played them and they were very repetitive. You basically shot stuff, went through cycles, and shot some more stuff, and so on and so on. There was no story *per se* and there was no real method by which you could create a story.

Veronese: How were you approached with the idea of *Atari Force* and working with Atari in general?

Conway: Jenette Kahn had the notion of synergy between Atari and DC Comics, and Jenette, Dick Giordano, Roy Thomas, and I went to a meeting in San Francisco with the Atari people. The meeting was all about cross pollinating between the two companies. I don't know who came up with the idea of *Atari Force, per se*, but we did think about it at those initial stages as a comic book that would be attached to the video games. The idea of developing it as a separate comic book came later, and I was interested in that because I am a science-fiction fan and I wanted to do a science-fiction-type series. Roy was less attracted to that sort of thing; *Swordquest* was more along the lines of something he was interested in. I don't even remember being that involved with *Swordquest* to be honest with you. Roy lucked out with getting George Pérez, and I lucked out with getting José Luis García-López. I'd love to see *Atari Force* collected one day, Jose did some amazing work.

Veronese: It seems like DC threw a large amount of talent at the Atari projects, with Gil Kane, Ross Andru, García-López, Pérez, Thomas, and yourself involved.

Conway: DC really gave it their top people, assuming you think Roy and I are top talent (laughs). DC also had contracts with Roy and I to produce a certain amount of writing on a regular basis, so it was to there advantage to put us on those projects. We were also writing films at that time, so that gave us a

great big bomb. We actually did have conversations with the developers who were concerned with the pressure they were under to churn games out before they were ready. I think they saw us as part of that problem and part of the pressure—to develop games that didn't necessarily have to exist. They knew the advantages and disadvantages of their platform, and they were being pressured by corporate suits to go beyond those constraints, and they very literally could not go past (the barrier) until a more sophisticated platform existed. By that point, however, PC gaming had taken hold and Atari was quickly left behind.

Veronese: You seem to have had some personal interest in computers. What was your background with computing?

Conway: I was a science-fiction fan, and the idea of having a personal computer was something that excited me. I owned a TRS-80 and I desperately wanted a TRS-80 Model 100, the mobile version. Roy Thomas and I wrote most of our screenplays on an Osborne 1 computer. I really wanted to be part of this world of the future that was developing before

certain amount of credibility. We were their media guys.

Veronese: You two were trans-media before there was trans-media.

Conway: Before the concept of trans-media even existed.

Veronese: Good point—the graphics were rudimentary and there was little voice audio at the time.

Conway: Yeah. From the developer's point of view it was sort of like trying to graft the head of a donkey onto the neck of a moose. They wondered what the point was in attempting to add a story. From our point of view, we didn't see anything we could add to a mix other than a marketing tool. It was, "Hey, buy this game and you get a free comic book." The *Swordquest* promotion combined completing four games and looking for clues in the comic book, but it was never completed as Atari went downhill very quickly. The *E.T.* game came out and…

Veronese: It was over.

Conway: Yeah, that was a

Opposite: (top to bottom)
Atari Force team

Atari Force #1

Above: (top to bottom)
Atari Force graphic novel,
interior page

Atari Force #5, interior page

our eyes. Atari was a major step forward at the time, as they actually had pixel animation, while most every other platform was text-based. The use of graphics opened up a whole new world, but the technology was still not advanced enough to take advantage of what we could bring into play story wise. When the graphics caught up, I did seek out story work in video games, but by then my television writing career took off and I sort of left that behind.

Veronese: Were there any other Atari projects that you worked on that never came to fruition?

Conway: Not that I recall. I know we were encouraged to find ways to do things with the other games that Atari had in development at the time—that's one of the reasons I used the word Tempest as one of the names of a character in *Atari Force*. In that sense, we were trying to come up with ways to reflect back. But really, *Atari Force* could have been named anything. Even the *Atari Force* comics included in the games really had no actual connection to Atari. There was no real identity to the material. If we had a greater sense of an Atari "concept" at the time, we might have come up with something. Each developer had their own approach as to how to develop games, and there really was no sense of "house style" like there was with later developers like Activision. These were just people desperately trying to meet deadlines and trying to not create something horrible.

Veronese: You hear stories of exceptionally crunched time frames for developers. It's a legend that the *E.T.* game was coded in 48 hours. Did you hear any other horror stories like that from your experience with Atari?

Conway: The *Swordquest* games themselves were under a crunch to develop even as there was no real sense of a game present. The developers were told to build a game around the concept of the presence of clues as part of a contest to win a prize. That's not the basis for a game, that's just not how you do things. Atari is a sort of tragic story; they made a ton of money off of a simple idea, *Pong*, creating a market for home video games, but they didn't have the console hardware to create something much more elaborate than *Pong*. But Atari had a ton of money,

and they went on a spending spree: the campus, the private gyms, everything that software developers would have later, but twenty years in the future. Atari also had the craziness of bringing in business people to run a company that should have been run by creative people. It was a mess. It was sad. Several people at the corporate level saw home console gaming as something of a fad, something with no legs, so they just wanted to make as much money as they could, as rapidly as they could.

Veronese: The idea of console gaming as a "fad" didn't really even go away until the late 1990s.

Conway: Very true. It wasn't seen as an art form, it was seen as something that had to be manipulated quickly. If you think about the early 1980s and video games, it was a lot like the early days of movie pro-

duction, where you had several "mom and pop" operations that became very valuable, but for no specific reason. Consumers who never thought they would be able to have the opportunity to play video games on their home television suddenly had the opportunity to do so. The people who created the technology may have seen the long-term viability, but the people who financed it did not; it was just a quick way to make money before it went bust. The market for arcade games was a boom-and-bust market, so it made sense for them to think that the console market might be as well, but it wasn't.

Veronese: I haven't even considered the arcade aspect of all this…

Conway: The arcade market was very big at the time. The movie *Tron* originated out of an arcade, it wasn't about a home video game. That's what the movie *The Last Starfighter* was about, the arcade games. The home video game market at the time was essentially an offshoot of the arcade market. The whole purpose of the arcade game is to get the player to put the next quarter in and the games had to be short. The purpose of the home game is to get you to buy something that is very expensive, but that will have replay ability over a long period of time. These are two totally different concepts. They had no real way to prepare for how to properly translate the arcade experience into a viable form of console gaming and the possibilities of additional storytelling.

Veronese: You mentioned PC gaming several times. Do you have any favorite games you have played over the years?

Conway: Oh sure. *Myst*, obviously, was a big influence on me. I loved the graphic puzzle solving games. *Wolfenstein, Doom* too. Once storytelling became a big part of games, I started following those, especially the first two *Resident Evil* games.

Veronese: I played hooky from school to play *Resident Evil* in 9th grade. That was the only time I ever played hooky.

Conway: Yeah, they are great, enthralling games with great stories. My biggest problem right now, is that I am aging, and my reflexes aren't what they once were. I'm very frustrated with console gaming now as the games seem to rely on how fast you can hit a button, and that is just not what I'm interested in. I'm interested exploring the world and the story; being taken on a journey. When I get frustrated that I can't move rapidly enough to make progress past a given point, I stop. I was talking to Marv Wolfman, who is also involved in video games, about adding a "storytelling" mode for those just interested in the story, but are unable to enjoy it. They would sell another 100,000 copies, easily, to people like me. That might be another marker that they are entirely missing.

Veronese: Nintendo has started a "story mode" with some of their recent Wii games, but still, those games have never been extremely story-oriented. But you have a great point, as a lot of recent games, like the *Uncharted* series, are very cinematic in nature.

Conway: There seems to be two conflicting impulses in a lot of modern games. The first would be an investment in the character and the story, a very genuine direction. The other is an impulse to play to the part of the brain that needs the endorphin kick that comes with beating a puzzle or a physical challenge. Those are two completely different parts of your brain though.

Veronese: And opposing parts of your brain even.

Conway: Yes, because one is about getting involved in a larger picture, putting together a story

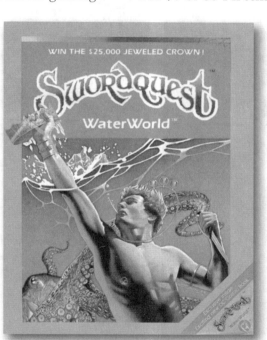

WIN THE $25,000 JEWELED CROWN!

Swordquest
WaterWorld

that moves forward and envelops the player, while the other is about needed gratification. I'm not sure if developers understand they are trying to create two very specific, very separate experiences. I don't play a lot of modern games because of this frustration and juxtaposition between difficulty and story, and I don't want to invest myself in something that I'll be annoyed by within a couple of hours. I feel like this medium of console gaming has left me behind, and now all I play is *World of Warcraft*, as that is something where I can meet the challenge and feel like I'm advancing.

Veronese: You bring up a really great point there, I turn 30 next month, and the video game systems in my house aren't going anywhere, and I suppose when I'm 70 or 80 I'll still have some sort of gaming device. I'll be in a retirement home somewhere at some point, maybe not even having full use of my appendages, but I'm sure I'll have the desire to play video games. I don't think I'm alone in this. Something will have to come along to fill this void, a market that caters to that situation.

Conway: Yeah, you would think. There are also people who cannot tolerate the first-person shooters, something that causes problems for a large part of your audience due to dizziness and spatial distortion. We're a fractionating society; we are no longer looking to go after the widest audience, but a very specific audience.

Veronese: And I'm like you, too, even now, where I've got better things to do than spend an hour trying to jump across a bridge. If it gets to that point, I'm selling the game or trading it in.

Conway: Exactly. When my frustration level rises above my entertainment level, I'm done. And if that happens on "easy" mode, I'm really done.

Veronese: I'm the same way. I'll pick up a book at that point; I'll at least get a story out the time and effort I've put forth.

Conway: Yeah, exactly. Show me a movie or give me another form of storytelling.

Opposite:
Swordquest #1

Below:
Swordquest: Waterworld game packaging

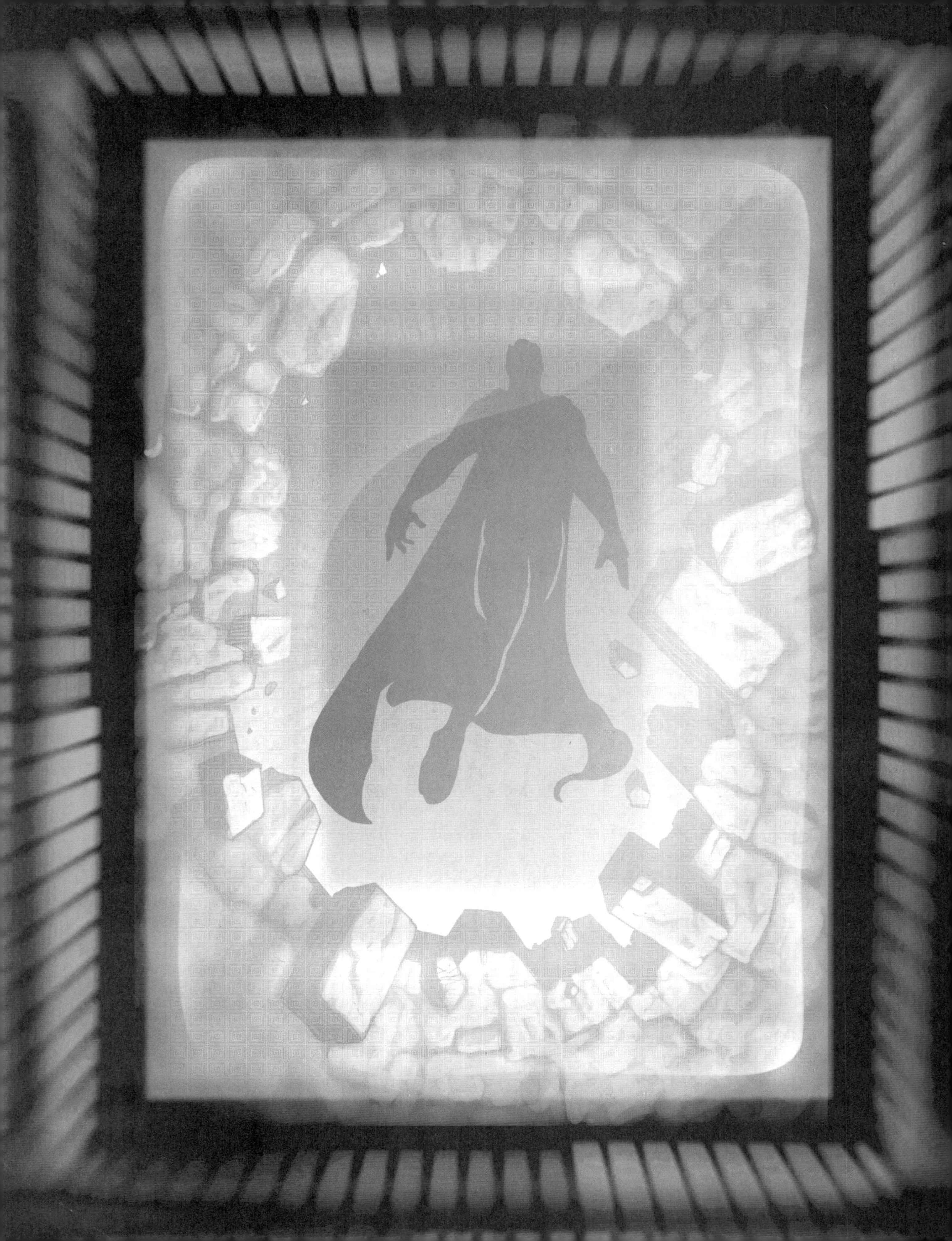

GAME**OVER?**

When dabbling in the world of video games, comic book artists are allowed to flex similar creative skills, fleshing out cutscenes or designing creatures for your enjoyment during gameplay.

Writers play a different role, writing dialogue, establishing the plot, or creating several-hundred-page documents—game "bibles" if you will—that lay down the entirety of a particular game's universe. Working with video game companies not only provides additional financial incentive, but exposure in additional genres. Whereas comic book artists might have dabbled in the commercial advertising field on the side in the 1960s and 1970s, modern comic book professionals can flex similar muscles and make more money in a creative environment by entering the video game industry.

Video games inspire a communal nature, with a Wednesday night game playing session or a regular set of online matches keeping lifelong friends in contact regardless of how far they are spread throughout the country. If the past three decades are any indicator, comic books and video games are two fields of entertainment that are here to stay, with current video game players likely holding controllers in their hands well into their time in a retirement home, with bingo tournaments replaced by *Halo* tournaments. After the tournament, I'll settle into my retirement home room and start back on my stack of graphic novels.

A single comic book and the twenty-two pages within takes the reader on a ten- to fifteen-minute journey, with a story arc or a pile of graphic novels taking up an entire afternoon. The reader sees a story from the joint perspective of an artist and a writer, while video games allow the gamer to become an active participant during a ten- to fifty-hour journey. These pastimes play to the passive and active forms of entertainment, complimenting each other and allowing for alternatives when a ten-hour video game binge is over and one is looking for something a little more cerebral.

Hopefully this book and the interviews within have opened your eyes to the work of artists and writers typically considered "comic book veterans" as they venture into the video game industry. Video games are an excellent bridge into the world of comic books and graphic novels, with tie-in comics often sold in retail stores next to their accompanying game or given away as pre-order bonuses. The "video game-based comic book" genre is a phenomenal resource, and one that should be cherished, as it places comic books in stores they would never garner shelf time within. Maybe some of these video game players turned comic book novices will enter their local comic book shop and be pulled into one of the greatest hobbies on earth.

Opposite:
Future game heroes?

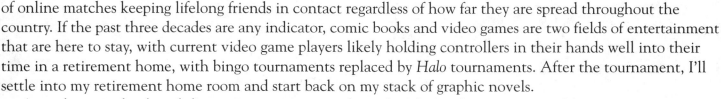

OTHER BOOKS FROM TWOMORROWS PUBLISHING

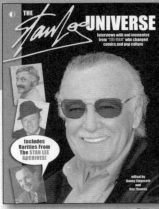

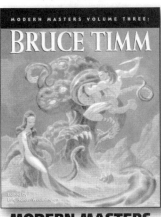

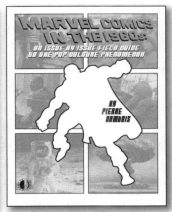
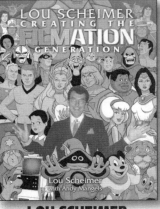